THE FLOWER OF MY

by the same author

ALMODÓVAR ON ALMODÓVAR
Edited by Frédéric Strauss

THE PATTY DIPHUSA STORIES AND OTHER WRITINGS

THE FLOWER
OF MY SECRET

Pedro Almodóvar

translated by
PETER BUSH

faber and faber
LONDON · BOSTON

First published in 1996
by Faber and Faber Limited
3 Queen Square London WC1N 3AU

Photoset by Parker Typesetting Service, Leicester
Printed in England by Clays Ltd, St Ives plc

© Pedro Almodóvar 1996

Translation © Peter Bush, 1996

Photographs of *Casablanca* and *Cat on a Hot Tin Roof* courtesy of BFI Stills,
Posters and Design. All other photographs courtesy of El Deseo S. A., Madrid

Pedro Almodóvar is hereby identified as author of this work in accordance with
Section 77 of the Copyright, Designs and Patents Act, 1988

A CIP record record for this book
is available from the British Library
ISBN 0-571-17870-7

2 4 6 8 10 9 7 5 3 1

CONTENTS

INT. THE MADRID COMMUNITY SCHOOL OF HOTEL
MANAGEMENT. DAY

*A small featureless space, enclosed by two or three screens forming a right
angle. There is an equally nondescript table, three chairs, and a curtain
on the wall.*

*This space is a corner of a Conference Room, separated off by the
screens. Altogether it's painfully ugly. A religious painting, quite by
chance, occupies a large area of one wall.*

*Two men dressed as doctors (in white coats) are sitting there. In the
following conversation, the two doctors talk unconvincingly, their
exaggerated concern highlights their play-acting (doctors aren't usually
that sensitive). The audience will assume they are bad actors. The third
chair is occupied by a woman who is fortyish, and as plain-looking as
the chairs and table. Throughout the scene the woman, Manuela, reacts
much more emphatically than the other two characters.*

DOCTOR A

We did everything we could, but your son Juan died . . .

MANUELA

It can't be true! I saw him a moment ago and he was breathing
. . . Haven't you made a mistake? You people do get things
wrong . . .

DOCTOR A

Not this time.

MANUELA

My Juan! I want to see him . . .

DOCTOR B

And you will . . . But first we must warn you not to go by
appearances . . . When you see him, you'll get the impression he's
breathing . . . But it's not true. It's the machines pumping oxygen
into him.

I

MANUELA
(*a little confused*)

Might he be in a coma?

DOCTOR B

No.

MANUELA
(*suddenly*)

I . . . if you don't mind, I'll take him elsewhere. I'll find the
money somehow . . . If there's the slightest possibility . . .

DOCTOR B

But there isn't, madam! Understanding brain death isn't easy . . .
(*he explains*)
We've got machines giving your son oxygen, that's why he looks as
if he's breathing. But his brain is dead.

MANUELA

Juan's very strong. He's only sixteen . . .
(*to Doctor B*)
If you say he looks as if he's breathing . . . he probably is . . .

DOCTOR A

It's the respirator . . . as my colleague explained to you . . .

MANUELA

I'm sorry, but I don't trust . . . The things you hear these days . . .
like the man who went in for an operation on his foreskin and was
given a vasectomy! It was in the newspapers . . .

DOCTOR B

Unfortunately we've got cast-iron proof . . . Juan's last EEG was
completely flat, and that means he's brain-dead . . .

Both doctors are showing signs of impatience.

MANUELA

I don't mind if he comes out a bit stupid, what matters is that he's
alive . . .

DOCTOR A
(categorically, almost rudely, wanting to settle the matter once and for all)

Madam, your son is dead!

MANUELA

Juan!

(covers her face with her hands)

DOCTOR A
(repeats)

. . . He died . . .

Pauses. He lets her take the news in.

Do you want us to inform any family?

MANUELA

I'm on my own. My husband died two years ago, a heart attack . . . there's my mother-in-law . . . but she's just a nuisance. She was the one who gave Juan the motorbike as a present . . . And I told him . . . if anything happens to you on the motorbike, it'll hit me even harder.

DOCTOR B

These things are an everyday occurrence . . .

MANUELA

Everyday? A son doesn't die on me everyday!

Suddenly, when she finally seems convinced, she looks at them even more intensely.

Swear to me!

The two doctors exchange bemused glances.

DOCTOR B

What?

MANUELA

Swear to me that my Juan is dead!

DOCTOR A

It's the first time we've been asked to do anything like that!

Doctor B understands how important it is to go along with her and avoid any kind of scene.

DOCTOR B

Yes, madam. We swear to it.

Manuela cries, hides her face in her hands. The doctors exchange glances again, and take advantage of the fact she can't see them to make an 'at last she's got it' gesture. An expression almost of liberation spreads over their faces.

For the first time the audience see that Manuela and the two doctors are not alone in the space divided off by the screens. In one corner there's a video camera (and a technician) recording the scene. None of the three looks at the camera. It's as if it doesn't really exist.

INT. CONFERENCE ROOM. THE MADRID COMMUNITY SCHOOL OF HOTEL MANAGEMENT. DAY

The image of Manuela with the two doctors can be seen on a video set up in the Conference Room.

Closed off by screens we now see that the opening sequence is taking place in a corner of a large square room, the windows of which face outside. Neutral, with plenty of light. Some twenty tables covered with a green cloth have been arranged, widely spaced out, in the centre of the room. Behind the tables are red chairs where young doctors sit, taking notes. Betty stands at the front next to a video monitor and flip-chart. Via the video the doctors and Betty can see everything happening in the closed-off space. This part of the room won't be shown till the end of the opening sequence.

Betty is a psychologist and nurse leading a seminar for doctors. The scene developed in the opening sequence is part of the practical for the seminar, and is merely the dramatization of a hypothetical, prototypical scene: how to communicate to a relative that a loved one has been killed in an accident.

Betty's friend and assistant, Manuela, is another nurse. She plays the role of the mother of a youth (Juan) who has suffered an accident so that the doctors can react appropriately. Manuela's play-acting isn't amateurish like the doctors'. Her imitation of an unhappy mother is

4

*quite lifelike. In fact, her interpretation initially confuses the audience –
everything is odd except for her. It is the decor that most jars; the bare
emptiness of the room hired out by the Madrid Community School for
Hotel Management.*

*The aim of the seminar is to teach doctors the most humane, the least
traumatic way to communicate the news of a sudden death to the
victim's relatives, in order to then ask them to donate the deceased's
organs.*

*The credits come up one after another in between these first two
sequences, with no fade-ins, fade-outs or slow fades. They give a rhythm
to the sequences without losing the thread of what is happening, because
the conversation can still be heard during the four or five seconds each
credit stays on screen.*

INT. LEO'S BEDROOM. DAY

*Meanwhile . . . Leo – forty something, good-looking, a youthful body
and an ominous look on her face – is asleep in bed; a bed that's too big
for a woman who lives alone. Leo sleeps embracing her pillow, her arms
and legs wrapped around it.*

*There are two piles of books on both levels of her bedside table. A photo
of Leo and her husband Paco, kissing, stands out from the top pile of
books. The frame of the photo is made of numerous blue marbles,
exquisitely designed, and was bought by Leo on one of her trips abroad.*

EXT. DAY

A shot of the sky, with or without reference to Leo's bedroom.

*A typically (wintry) Madrid sky, threateningly grey with rays of light
raking up over the backs of the clouds.*

A sky heralding stormy weather.

INT. LEO'S BEDROOM.

*A strong wind blows the window to Leo's bedroom open. The gust hits
the open pages of* She Imagines, *a book by Juan José Millás, on the
floor, next to the bed, and quickly turns them over with an invisible
finger.*

The edge of one page is folded over in the shape of a triangle and a phrase has been underlined: 'Defenceless and a prey to madness.' The book had 'defenceless' in the Spanish masculine form, indefenso, but Leo has appropriated that defencelessness by putting a circle round it and writing the feminine form, indefensa.

The tap-tap of a typewriter keyboard.

INT. LEO'S STUDY. DAY

In the part of the house that Leo devotes to her work. Walls lined with shelves full of books. A desk bathed in light from the window overlooking a school playground in a humdrum district of Madrid.

Leo types out:

'Defenceless and a prey to madness'
'Defenceless and a prey to madness'
'Defenceless and a prey to madness'

Leo reads the phrase aloud several times. The book is next to her typewriter, open at the page with the underlined phrase. There are more books lying open with phrases or words encircled. And on the sheet of paper, preceding that phrase, there are several phrases, also repeated. It's a memorizing exercise rather than an obsession. Though Leo's actions reflect a bit of both . . .

'sad shock . . .'
'sad shock . . .'
'sad shock . . .'
'irritable looking'
'irritable looking'
'trick, trick, trick'
'trick, trick, trick'

Though she has a word-processor on her desk, Leo prefers using a typewriter with a daisy-wheel (or a golf-ball). She likes the sound it makes. She's got used to it. The tap-tap of the keys keeps her company.

The camera, after showing us the first line of 'Defenceless . . .' pans over the messy array of objects that fill the top of the desk. Diverse containers for pens; Fornassetti ashtrays; notebooks from various countries – some new, others half-used – all with titles written in Dymo

6

marker-pen (for example. 'Plans', 'Phrases', 'Cuttings', 'Quotations' etc.). Leo's obsessed by Dymo pens and yellow Post-its. The table and shelves are covered in Post-its stuck on to form a fringe.

On the table, there are also bottles of medicine. Books with lots of markers sticking out. Folders. One folder, headed 'Cuttings' in Dymo-size letters, stands out. On the top of the folder there are various bits of newspaper of varying sizes and from a wide range of sources that have yet to be organized or filed. The first, from El Mundo, *relates the suicide of Kurt Cobain. The headline reads: 'More than my share of suffering'. The headline is also underlined, or circled.*

After the shot panning over the table (there are also glasses, whose contents were consumed the day before, and the odd bottle), the sound of the sheet of paper being taken from the typewriter can be heard. Leo inserts a fresh sheet. We hear its contents in a voice-over, as if Leo were reading it aloud (her inner voice). Sometimes Leo speaks to herself through the typewriter. On the table, submerged in paper, there's also a small, exquisitely framed photo of Paco.

LEO
(*voice-over*)

Everyday I wear something from you . . .

She looks at his photo.

Today I'm wearing the ankle boots you gave me two years ago. Do you remember how at night you had to take them off, because I was unable to by myself? When I saw them this morning I was reminded of you and put them on in your honour. They're too tight now. Sometimes, like these boots, the memory of you weighs heavily on my heart, prevents me from breathing. I'd better take them off.

(*to herself*)

I'm beginning to get depressed.

Leo's hair is pinned back, she's wearing almost no make-up. And looks neat and restrained. She's in shirt and trousers. And the boots her text refers to.

Leo stops writing. She moves her chair back, away from the table, and tries to take her boots off. She can't. She tries several times but with no success.

7

As if levered by a hidden spring, she goes back to her desk. And resumes her jottings. Her voice-over continues.

I can't take them off!

The effort makes her feel lonely and defenceless. She kicks the floor once, in a fit of rage.

INT. LEO'S HOUSE. DAY

Leo dials a telephone number and waits for a response at the other end of the line.

INT. A REHEARSAL ROOM. DAY

In the corridor off the room, a telephone on the wall keeps ringing but nobody picks it up.

A rented room. A wooden floor, white walls, a big mirror on one wall, and a scattering of rush chairs. A typical dance rehearsal room.

Accompanied by clapping from his mother Blanca, and others in the group, Antonio stamps his heels on the floor. There's also a gypsy, pounding a drum.

The drumming, clapping and heel-stamping create such a din that it's

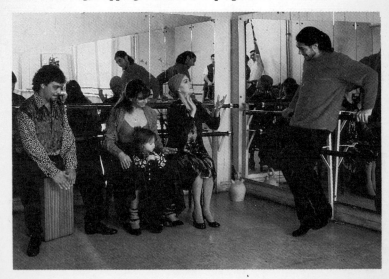

8

impossible to hear the telephone still ringing in a nearby corridor.

*Blanca: lithe and serious, an Andalusian with eternal Greek looks.
Between forty-five and fifty years old. Antonio, the youth, is dark and
handsome like his mother. But when he stamps his feet, he's
transfigured, glows. Together they make an explosive, original couple.*

INT. LEO'S HOUSE. DAY

A dispirited Leo puts the phone down.

INT. A REHEARSAL ROOM. DAY

In the corridor, the bell stops ringing.

*At that very moment, Blanca and her son stop stamping their heels in
order to discuss the dance routine.*

*That morning the world of heels seems to have conspired against the
fragile Leo.*

EXT. STREET. DAY

*Grey and depressing, the day drags on. Some large drops of rain start to
fall. The threat of rain catches Leo out in the street, but she doesn't feel
like going home for an umbrella.*

*As she stands on the pavement, Leo's anguished eyes reach along to the
end of the street. No unoccupied taxis.*

*She starts walking. She's carrying a plastic bag containing shoes. Still
wearing the oppressive boots.*

*She's accosted by a young junkie begging. He wants a thousand pesetas.
To begin with Leo looks at him apprehensively and ignores his plea, but
the junkie follows close behind, explaining in servile tones that he's not
intent on aggression, he only wants a thousand pesetas. Leo stops and
squares up to him in determined fashion.*

LEO

If you help me get these boots off, I'll give you five thousand pesetas.

*Far from being surprised by such a strange proposition, the junkie
welcomes it enthusiastically.*

9

JUNKIE

You're on, rightaway!

LEO

Haven't we met somewhere before?

JUNKIE

I don't think so . . .

Leo sits on the step of a fountain in a square and offers up her leg to the exhausted drug addict. Leo indicates to the weak, fumbling youth how to get the boot off.

LEO

Hold on to the heel and pull . . .

The junkie does as he's told, but doesn't get the boot to budge a centimetre. It starts to rain. Neither seems worried. Leo reclaims her foot.

LEO

Look, do it like this, pull on the heel; and push the toe downwards. But please get a move on . . . You're going to get soaked . . .

JUNKIE

Don't worry . . . I like the rain . . .

The youth makes repeated attempts, putting all his energy into it. For him, those five thousand pesetas are a matter of life and death. Sweat and rain pour down his face and hair. In the end the scene makes Leo ill.

LEO

Let go . . .

Leo recovers her foot.

JUNKIE
(*a suggestion*)

I'll get a friend and between the two of us. . .

LEO
(*gets up and hands over a note*)

Don't worry, here you are.

Before the junkie dissolves in an effusion of gratitude, Leo disappears into the rain, worn to a frazzle.

INT. BAR. DAY

An ordinary bar in the area. Ethnic music from a jukebox gives the place a contagious cheerfulness. A wide range of food and fruit-machines. Leo (her hair and clothes sopping wet) asks the waiter behind the bar for a coffee with a dash of cognac. She drinks it quickly, it helps her gather herself together. Then she slots coins into a telephone installed on the wall.

At the other end of the line a voice replies:

VOICE

National Transplant Organization!

LEO

Hello, I'm Leo, Betty's friend. Can I talk to her?

VOICE

She's not here, she's off giving one of her seminars . . .

11

LEO

Please, can you tell me where?

VOICE

In the Madrid Community School for Hotel Management.

LEO

Right, the usual place . . .

VOICE

Yes. I imagine she won't be finished till the evening . . .

LEO

Thank you.

She hangs up.

She looks thoughtful, glances around her. Could she perhaps ask any of the bar's clientèle to help take off her boots? She doesn't think that wise.

There's a noisy, cheerful atmosphere in the bar, as if the rain had put everybody in a good mood. But it doesn't manage to reach out to Leo, her anguish is a kind of micro-climate enveloping her alone.

INT. CONFERENCE ROOM AND CORNER IN THE SCHOOL OF HOTEL MANAGEMENT

The continuation of the opening sequence. The same layout. The same doctors A and B pursuing their conversation with Manuela, around the same table. This sequence is seen alternately where it is happening and on the video next to Betty, in the middle of the Conference Room.

DOCTOR A

Did your son have a generous soul? Did he worry about social problems . . . ?

MANUELA

I don't know . . . He wanted to become a conscientious objector . . . he was against violence, war . . . and quite right too . . .

DOCTOR A
(*pressing her rather*)
That means he was worried about other . . .

DOCTOR B
(*takes it as given*)

Of course . . . !

DOCTOR A

Did you talk about death a lot?

MANUELA

Why would he talk about death? He was only sixteen!

DOCTOR B
(*changes tack*)

We mention this because there are people who decide to donate their organs while they're alive . . . and . . . we wanted to know whether Juan . . .

MANUELA
(*interrupting him*)

Are you going to do a transplant? Do you think something can still be done?

DOCTOR B

A lot can be done, but not for your son, for other sick people.

DOCTOR A

Don't misunderstand us. But your son's organs could save lots of lives . . .

DOCTOR B

In the case of Juan, where everything is useable because he was so young and healthy, five lives.

DOCTOR A

But we need your authorization for that . . .

MANUELA
(*rejects this, looks appalled*)

Don't make me suffer any more. A lady in the waiting-room had already tipped me off. You can't ask me to mutilate my son . . .

DOCTOR A

It's not mutilation . . . just a simple internal operation . . . he won't look any different.

MANUELA

I want to see my son!

DOCTOR A

Think it over . . . Eighty per cent of relatives consulted give permission, and find it very consoling . . . I can tell you from experience . . .

The woman tries to calm down and think.

In the Conference Room, Betty and the other doctors in the seminar are watching the drama on the video monitor. Some take notes.

MANUELA

Who would you give the organs to?

DOCTOR B

To whoever needs them most . . .

MANUELA

You wouldn't ever give them to an Arab, for example?

DOCTOR B
(*that's the last thing he'd expected to hear*)

To an Arab? . . . To the person most in need, whatever their race or social position . . .

MANUELA

I've read there are these wealthy Arabs who buy everything up.

DOCTOR B
(*annoyed*)

Madam, that happens in Third World countries . . . In Spain we belong to the European Plan for Organ Donation and everything is completely above board.

Manuela takes this information in.

MANUELA

At least they'll stay in Madrid?

DOCTOR B

The law on transplants doesn't allow us to divulge that information . . .

MANUELA
(*at a loss*)
I don't know . . . Can't you wait a few days . . . ? I'm not in a fit
state to think . . .

DOCTOR B
We can't wait. Unfortunately, there's not time . . . You have only
a few minutes to decide . . .

DOCTOR A
(*correcting Doctor B*)
Take whatever time you need . . . and if we can help you sort out
any problems, let us know . . . We aren't just here to ask for
organs, but to offer you help . . . I'm sorry, that's how we should
have started . . .

*Manuela is animated, talking to herself, but as a nurse now, not the
mother.*

MANUELA
It's never too late . . . Come on, let's go . . .

INT. THE CONFERENCE ROOM. THE SCHOOL OF HOTEL
MANAGEMENT. DAY

*Manuela, Doctors A and B finish off their dramatization behind the
screens. They get up and leave the nondescript table to join the other
people attending the seminar.*

*As previously described, in the centre of the Conference Room, twenty
doctors of both sexes and of diverse ages, sit on red chairs in a U shaped
formation, lean on tables covered in green cloth, and follow the seminar
Betty is leading.*

*The psychologist stands in front of the group, closing off the U. She is
flanked by the monitor broadcasting live (and in playback) the events
behind the screens, a small screen for slide projection, and a flip-chart.
There are cards with the participants' first names on the tables.*

Everyone uses tú, *the familiar Spanish word for 'you', though the
informality seems contrived.*

While Manuela and the doctors come through (on the video we have seen them get up and leave the space behind the screens). Betty, all smiles, rewinds the video.

> BETTY
> (*to Manuela*)

Manuela, you were marvellous.

The two doctors (A and B) join the rest of the participants and return to their part of the U formation. Manuela remains standing, next to Betty.

> MANUELA

Thanks, but I reckon I was a bit weepy . . .

> BETTY

Not at all! Every seminar you turn in a better performance . . .
> (*to the doctors who have just done the dramatization*)

If you have any comments, tell me and I'll stop the video. What about you, Roberto.
> (*she looks at Doctor A*)

How did you feel?

> DOCTOR A

Terrible, especially when Manuela refused to understand about brain death.

> MANUELA
> (*protesting*)

Look, I didn't refuse. Forget that I'm a nurse. There are lots of people who don't even know what an EEG is.

> BETTY

Brain death isn't easy to explain, or understand. At times like these a relative suffers from 'bereavement crisis', and is ready to grab any scrap of hope, however pathetic. You can't talk about donations until the relative has understood and accepted the death, and for that to happen it must be explained very clearly and very respectfully.

INT. MADRID COMMUNITY SCHOOL OF HOTEL MANAGEMENT

Without anyone noticing, the door to the room opens a few centimetres allowing a glimpse of Leo's face just at the moment when Betty is talking about 'bereavement crisis'. She listens, then closes the door.

CORRIDOR

She sits on a sofa by the door. In the area facing the corridor there's a display stand with the name of the course Betty is leading: 'An Integral Approach to Organ Donation.'

INT. CONFERENCE ROOM. DAY

Betty finishes rewinding the video tape. She turns to Doctor B.

> BETTY

How about you, Fernando?

> DOCTOR B

I couldn't have been worse . . .

> BETTY

At the end you weren't bad. But that's where you should have started; by offering to help.
> (*to the others*)

Your mission is to help the family, reduce the tension produced by news of the death, and smooth the way to a donation. Notice how I said smooth the way and not 'get' . . .
> (*turns to Doctor B*)

What was the worst moment for you?

> DOCTOR B

The Arab business. I was furious, I couldn't help it.

> BETTY

Because you were 'judging' Manuela's reaction.

> MANUELA

Come on, Betty. Not mine, the mother's. I'm no racist.

> BETTY

I know.

(*to Doctor B*)

Your rejection was entirely reasonable. But you can't 'judge' the relative. That's basic. Pain and fear justify any reaction, even the crudest sort.

INT. CORRIDOR. OUTSIDE DOOR TO CONFERENCE ROOM. DAY

The seminar members talk about the incidents as they walk out of the door. Betty leaves with Manuela. She spots Leo sitting on a chair, waiting. Surprised to see her there, she immediately realizes her friend has got problems.

BETTY

Leo, what are you doing here?

Leo, bewildered, shame-faced, overcome by her awareness that she's totally in the way.

LEO

I needed to see you . . . I know you're very busy . . . But I promise it'll only take a minute . . .

Betty says goodbye to Manuela.

BETTY

Manuela, wait for me in the cafeteria.

Manuela says hallo to Leo. They know each other. Manuela is no longer acting the mother, she's a nurse, and younger than she appeared in the dramatization. She's probably changed her hairstyle (loose, not gathered up).

MANUELA

Is something really wrong, Leo?

LEO

No. It's just raining . . .
(*feigns a smile*)
I must talk to Betty for a minute . . .

Manuela leaves them alone.

LEO

Where can we be by ourselves?

18

This way . . . follow me.

Betty takes Leo into the by now empty Conference Room.

Somewhat younger than Leo, Betty oozes self-confidence. She has everything worked out. She's attractive if rather cold. That firmness, lack of fault-lines, is what makes her seem cold, even though she isn't. Perhaps it's all to do with her hairstyle . . . That smooth, blonde, shoulder-length hair.

Dynamic, modern and genuinely worried by the social problems she sees around her. Sometimes her sense of concern can be mistaken for interference in other people's lives. She wears expensive but discreet clothes that dilute the possible impact of her beauty.

Leo conceals her damp, sad eyes behind dark glasses which give her an air of mystery.

Betty, on the other hand, wears glasses with transparent lenses in order to see things clearly. These lenses make her look more respectable.

Leo sits down in one of the armchairs one of the doctors has just vacated. Betty looks at her cautiously.

BETTY

Well . . . what's the matter?

LEO
(*stammering*)
You'll think I'm a fool, but . . .
(*threatening to burst into tears*)
I came so you could help me take my boots off. By myself . . . I
. . . couldn't . . .

Betty gives her a withering look as if to say 'And was that why you had the cheek to interrupt me in full flow?' But she says nothing, restrains herself.

I've no one to turn to. It's Blanca, my maid's, day off . . . I called but couldn't get her . . .
(*bursts into tears*)

Betty, hiding her amazement as best she can, tries to appear caring and natural.

19

Come on, give me that foot.

Leo stretches her foot out, Betty takes the boot and starts pulling. It doesn't come off easily. Her hair becomes slightly ruffled. (This makes her furious, but she also hides this.)

LEO
(*explains*)
A present from Paco two years ago. At night, in the hotel, he had to take them off . . . because I couldn't by myself . . .

A fresh outbreak of sobbing, brought on by the tender memory of her absent husband.

Betty makes a big effort and takes both boots off. It leaves her exhausted. She turns to look at her friend. Leo takes a pair of shoes from her bag and puts them on. Betty watches the operation while tidying her hair back into place, and avoids all comment. But it's obvious the scene has upset her more than one would expect, considering she's a psychologist.

Thanks, Betty.

BETTY
Leo . . . you can't carry on like this.

LEO
(*ingenuously*)
Like what?

BETTY
Crying over every little thing . . .

LEO
What do you expect me to do . . . ?

Realizes Betty is in the middle of a work-session and changes tone.

OK, I won't keep you any longer. I'm off . . .

She gets up in the direction of the door. Betty looks at her, feels upset and guilty.

Can't we meet for dinner this evening?

LEO
If you can, I'd be delighted . . .

They kiss each other goodbye. Leo turns round before she reaches the door.

And don't worry about me, I'm not that bad . . .

She closes the door. Betty's left standing alone in the empty room. She puts her hands in her trouser pockets, looks anxious.

INT. RESTAURANT. NIGHT

One of those special Madrid restaurants. Simple but full of charm, an expensive kind of tavern, its walls full of life and bottles.

Betty and Leo are eating together. Leo's in better spirits, thanks to a bottle of wine, now nearing its end. She has dressed for the occasion. Neither is wearing glasses, and both look more attractive.

LEO
(*commenting*)
Betty, if I keep drinking I'll turn myself into an alcoholic anonymous.

BETTY
Did you go to see my friend Angel at *El País*?

LEO

Not yet.

BETTY
Aren't you interested anymore?

LEO
I am . . . but it's embarrassing . . . turning up . . . out of the blue . . .

BETTY
Don't be silly! Angel's a sweetie, and a very close friend of mine. Promise you'll go tomorrow or the day after.

LEO
All right. Have you told him who I am?

No . . . you tell him, if you think it's the right moment.

A waiter walks past their table, to serve other customers. Besides eating, the two women despatch the bottle of wine with gusto. Leo drinks more, and at greater speed than Betty.

Oh Betty, apart from drinking, I find everything so difficult!

Leo, you've got to get out of the house, do things. You can't spend the whole day waiting for Paco to ring.

What do you think I should do?

React positively. If you're not able to do so by yourself, tell me and we'll get specialist help.

I don't need a specialist, I need Paco . . .

Leo, you're not the first woman to have problems with her husband.

That's no consolation.

INT. LEO'S HOUSE. STUDY. DAY

Leo's searching among the mess of folders, notebooks, opened books, etc. This continues in various parts of the study, also littered with notebooks and folders. Evidently, she doesn't find what she's after. She picks up an envelope with a 200 page volume and a small folder with two separately stapled articles, full of crossings out. Fleetingly we see the title of one of the articles. 'The pain of living'.

Far away, in the kitchen, the sound of flamenco. Her maid is listening to the radio.

INT. LEO'S HOUSE. KITCHEN. DAY

In the kitchen, Blanca is ironing clothes (or peeling potatoes) while listening to flamenco on the radio-cassette player. It's the same woman we saw in the rehearsal room, who works here as a maid. Leo appears, somewhat in a rush.

> BLANCA

Can I help look for something?

> *Leo looks at her, taken aback. As far as Blanca is concerned, it's a routine question. Blanca speaks with a broad, Andalusian accent. There is a clear class difference between her and Leo.*

What have you lost today?

> LEO

I don't know . . . I'm looking for two files like this
> (*shows her*)
with wads of sheets inside. I did a fair copy last week. They must be somewhere . . . but why should you know!

> BLANCA

Have you looked in your study?

> LEO

It's impossible to find anything there.

> BLANCA

If only you hadn't ordered me not to tidy your table up . . . ! Let me have a look . . .

> LEO

It's got 'Articles' written on the cover . . .

INT. LEO'S HOUSE. LOUNGE. DAY

Blanca walks towards the lounge and looks among the magazines on the centre-table; literary and fashion magazines, plus recent cuttings. There's a big A4-size folder on the mantelpiece. She looks inside. Finds two files that are green cardboard, not plastic. Just in case, she picks them up and hands them to Leo.

BLANCA

Are these them? They're not plastic . . . but it says 'Articles'.

LEO

That's them . . . you're so clever, Blanca!
(*suddenly, thoughtful*)
There was something I had to tell you . . .

She tries to remember but can't.

INT. LEO'S HOUSE. KITCHEN. DAY

Leo goes with Blanca into the kitchen.

BLANCA

Take a phosphorous tablet.

She fills a glass of water and hands it to Leo with the pill.

LEO

It won't get me my memory back, but it does make me as randy as a bitch. Did you know phosphorous is an aphrodisiac?

BLANCA

What does that mean?

LEO
(*as she takes it*)

Oh . . . I remember. If my husband telephones ask him to please ring back tonight. If he asks how I am, lie and tell him I'm really feeling great.

Blanca nods to all this. Leo throws the two old files, that are full of crossings-out, into the rubbish bin. Someone rings the bell on the backdoor that leads straight into the kitchen.

BLANCA

That'll be Antonio, I told him to bring the bottles . . . so I didn't have such a load . . .

They both go over to the door. Open it.

Leo and Antonio say hello. Antonio's carrying two bags with different kinds of bottles. He's the youth who was dancing in the rehearsal room. Leo gives him a warm welcome.

24

In Leo's presence, the youth behaves timidly, as if inhibited. Before closing the door, Leo says goodbye to both mother and son.

Antonio takes the bottles out of their bags. Solán de Cabras mineral water, beer, Coca-cola and two bottles of whisky, several of ginger ale, gin etc. He talks to his mother, as he puts them inside the fridge. Blanca is probably peeling potatoes for a Spanish omelette. During the whole conversation she keeps on one spot, and finishes off what she's doing. Antonio, however, once he's put the bottles away, closes the fridge and walks over to the other side of the kitchen and pours himself a coffee, freshly made in an English coffee-maker.

ANTONIO
(*coarsely*)
She don't eat much, but drink! She gets pissed.

BLANCA
Writers drink a lot . . .

ANTONIO
So do drunks!

BLANCA
Antonio
(*reproaching him*)
I don't like you mouthing off about her!

ANTONIO
All right . . . have you told her yet?

BLANCA
No . . .

ANTONIO
What are you waiting for?

BLANCA
I can't leave her now, when the poor thing most needs me.

ANTONIO
Mam . . . we can't miss this chance. I don't know when we'll get another.

BLANCA

What chance? I'll believe that when I see the contract!

ANTONIO

The only thing I'm asking you to do is rehearse. I'll see to the rest . . .

BLANCA

That's what worries me. I don't understand a producer who's not seen a thing, giving you two million . . .

(*changes her tone*)

Come on, take the dustbin down.

Antonio goes over to the dustbin, avoids giving an answer, and takes out the files with the two articles that are full of corrections. One's entitled 'The Pain of Living'.

Perhaps he wants something from you in exchange?

ANTONIO

(*protesting*)

What do you mean!

After glancing at the files, he puts them back in the rubbish bag. And closes it.

BLANCA

Antonio, why don't you find someone else? I've not danced in years. My back's done in!

ANTONIO

Don't start, mam . . .

(*emphatically*)

You're the best!

BLANCA

Was the best. And a long time ago.

She carries on peeling potatoes by the draining-board.

EXT. THE FRONT OF THE *EL PAÍS* BUILDING. DAY

Leo looks at the façade topped by the name El País as David would look at Goliath, at once fearful and defiant. She walks into the building.

26

INT. THE *EL PAÍS* BUILDING. FOURTH FLOOR. DAY

Leo reaches the place where Angel is standing with a friend. From there one can see the newspaper's modern, sophisticated rotary press. Angel is proudly showing it off to his friend, with an air of childish wonder, as if pointing out some out-of-the-ordinary monorail electric train. The artefact in motion is really spectacular and impressive. Leo also looks on in awe.

Angel is a young, plumpish, friendly fellow who's quite a character and fond of his drink. He's sentimental and extrovert. An ironic guy who hides his loneliness and despair behind his amusing excesses. His implacable irony makes him sometimes seem prickly and snobbish, cruel and self-punishing. But it's obvious this exterior conceals a bleeding heart hungry for love.

Leo is sombre, fragile, mysterious: a cancer of the emotions has been gradually undermining her self-confidence. However, that kind of continuous crisis can make her very daring, in certain circumstances. Sometimes she reacts with the courage of someone with nothing to lose.

Angel says goodbye to his friend. Inevitably Leo and Angel look at each other while the rotary press roars away. Although he doesn't know Leo, Angel approaches her.

27

ANGEL

Hello . . .

LEO

Hello. I'm Leo Macías . . . Betty's friend.

ANGEL
(*pleasantly surprised*)

Oh, so you're . . . ? Betty rang to tell me you'd be coming. How
can I help?

*They start walking and leave the big room with the rotary press. It
would have been impossible to talk with that noise.*

LEO

Well . . . the truth is, I am being rather bold.

*She says this with a shy but charming smile. They walk towards
Angel's office.*

INT. A GLASS-PANELLED CORRIDOR. DAY

*They carry on talking as they walk down a very wide corridor. Lift
doors are on one side, and on the other a large array of tables, behind
which the staff of the newspaper sit: the human machinery, less noisy
but equally frantic in its activity. Sub-divided into smaller units, the
space is full of people writing on their word-processors or answering the
telephone.*

Leo gazes at the panorama (an updated version of the big office in The
Apartment) *quite entranced.*

LEO

I would like to write for your newspaper . . .
(*specifies*)

about literature . . .

*She finds it quite an effort to broach the subject, she imagines Angel is
only too familiar with the routine of the typical woman after the main
chance. If that's so, he does well to hide the fact; he looks at Leo
warmly, curious. It's not surprising he likes her. Leo looks her best for
the occasion: an interesting woman of indeterminate age, cultured,
with an air of mystery.*

28

(shamefaced, but persuasive)
I'm a writer . . . But above all a very good reader. I could write
literary criticism . . . or write books. I warned you I would be
bold.

ANGEL
The supplement could do with an injection of boldness. I'm trying
to lighten it a little. By the way, I'm not sure I've ever read
anything by you.

LEO
(forcefully)
No. You haven't read a word.

ANGEL
How do you know?
(jokingly)
Do I look uncultured?

LEO
No. It's just that I haven't published anything.

ANGEL
Oh!

LEO
(explaining herself)
Obviously I don't expect you to give me work because I'm
Beatriz's friend. I've brought you a few things, so you can get an
idea about my writing.

> *They reach the door to Angel's office. There's a plate with his name*
> *and position at the top: Editor-in-Chief of the Cultural Supplement.*
> *While she looks at that sign, Leo takes some files from her bag, two*
> *small ones and a thicker one, about 200 pages (the novel). She hands*
> *them over to Angel.*

> *He is both intrigued and attracted by the woman. In spite of the*
> *unusual nature of the situation, Leo acts quite reasonably.*

All right, I don't want to waste any more of your time. Thanks for
listening . . .

You're not wasting anything at all. Could we continue the conversation in my office?

LEO

Fine.

Leo looks at him, surprised by his invitation. She didn't think Angel would give her so much time. However . . .

I must go to the lavatory.

Angel points to a door inside. (If there isn't a lavatory inside, Angel tells her how to get to the nearest one.)

INT. A LAVATORY. DAY

She looks at her face in the mirror. For the moment, no repair work necessary. She takes a small hipflask from her bag and has a swig. Has another look in the mirror, pulls the chain and leaves.

INT. ANGEL SERRANO'S OFFICE. DAY

She finds Angel at one end of the office. It's a very sobre space, with few personal touches. There's a coffee-making machine on a side table; he

offers Leo a cup. She accepts and sits down. Angel pours her a cup and
takes another for himself. He sits down opposite Leo and, trying to
bridge the gap, he takes a small bottle of whisky from one of the
drawers, pours some into his coffee and with a wave offers Leo some.
She smiles and declines the offer.

Whilst they drink from their respective cups, Angel reads the title on the
biggest file.

> ANGEL

'The Cold Store'. Is it a novel you've written?

> LEO

Yes . . . Of course . . .

> *An atmosphere of trust. Angel and Leo feel much more relaxed than*
> *at the beginning.*

> ANGEL

As it's not signed . . .

> LEO

I forgot . . .

> ANGEL

When did you start writing?

> LEO

I must have been about ten years old. My family moved to
Extramadura for economic reasons. We lived in a street of
illiterates. The neighbours used to come to our house, and I'd
write their letters for a few pesetas . . . and read the ones they
received. Since then I've not stopped reading, or writing.

> ANGEL

How wonderful the school of life can be.

> LEO

Sometimes, in the summer, when they were enjoying the cool in
the doorway to the street, I would read novels to my female
neighbours.

> ANGEL

What kind of novels?

LEO
(*shamefaced*)
Romantic novelettes . . . But I'm talking about when I was a
young girl.

ANGEL
Have you specialized in a particular genre, issue or period?

On the table are two piles of recently published books by various authors.
The top one is an Amanda Gris anthology. Leo spots it, by chance.

LEO
No. But I would prefer to write only about what I like, and if I can
avoid Spanish literature so much the better. Oh, and something
else . . .

ANGEL
(*smiles*)
Any other conditions?

LEO
Yes, I'd like to have a pseudonym as a by-line.

Angel feels more and more intrigued by this woman. He's fascinated
by her blend of daring and timidity.

ANGEL
Very well. But give me some idea . . . which writers do you like?

LEO
Mostly women. Adventurers, suicides. Neurotics. Victims of
themselves . . . and of the society of their time. For example,
Djuna Barnes, Jane Bowles, Dorothy Parker, Jean Rhys, Flannery
O'Connor, Virginia Woolf, Edith Wharton, Isak Dinesen, Janet
Frame . . .

ANGEL
Quite a bunch!

LEO
One of the articles
(*pointing at the files*)
is about them . . . That's why I reeled off their names parrot-
fashion . . . They're very much on my mind . . .

32

I'm also very interest in literature by women . . . What do you make of Amanda Gris?

Leo looks at him as if he'd just sniped at her, or was making fun of her. She reacts quite clumsily.

LEO

How do you know Amanda Gris is a woman?

ANGEL
(*at a loss*)

Well . . .

LEO

Nobody's ever seen a photo of her. Nobody knows who she is!

ANGEL

Now you mention it, you're right. But the genre she writes in is typically for women . . . from Barbara Cartland to Venezuelan soaps.

Leo looks at him daggers drawn.

I can see you don't like love and romance novelettes.

LEO

Right. But I think the literature you're referring to doesn't touch on real romance at all. There's no pain or heartache. Only cliché, self-satisfaction and sentimentality.

ANGEL

I respect your opinion, but disagree. Would you like to develop what you've just said over five pages of A4?

LEO

I'm afraid I'm not the right person. Amanda Gris disgusts me.

ANGEL

Better still. On subjects of this nature we like publishing a column against and one in favour. Obviously, you'd get first shot.

LEO
(*drily*)

I don't like writing against. I've got enough that's negative in my

33

world. I don't want to add any extra and much less be paid for the pleasure. Goodbye.

After saying this, in the sincerest possible tone and not wishing to deliver a moral lecture, Leo gets up. She makes as if to collect up her files. Angel anticipates her reaction, puts his hands on Leo's and pulls the files to the end of the table nearest to him. Leo looks him in the face, as if to ask him what he's playing at. Angel is also very sincere in his apologies:

ANGEL
(*quite spontaneously*)
I'm sorry, I get very clumsy with people I like.

Leo is more affected than she'd like to admit. Looks at the table, as if at a loss.

LEO
I don't understand you!

Angel is afraid she'll burst into tears.

ANGEL
Forget it! There's no need to write about Amanda Gris. I'll read what you've brought me and ring you in a couple of days. But don't look at me like that.

Angel speaks in a serious tone.

LEO
(*hesitantly*)
All right, then. Goodbye.

She turns round, walks to the door, opens it, goes out, closes it. Angel has watched her every movement. As Leo closes the door, he says to himself:

ANGEL
I'm a real bastard!

EXT. AROUND THE *EL PAÍS* BUILDING. THE STREET

Leo wipes away a few tears. Puts some dark glasses over her eyes. Her first incursion into the world outside couldn't have been more upsetting.

34

A musical theme starts up, and continues in the following sequence.

EXT. A ROAD LEADING TO THE OUTSKIRTS. EARLY AFTERNOON

Leo's driving her car. Probably listening to the radio or a cassette. She's not looking at the view. She knows it by heart, or is simply absorbed in her own thoughts. She's changed clothes. Two plastic bags full of clothes are on the seat next to her.

EXT. THE OUTER RIM. A NEIGHBOURHOOD ON THE OUTSKIRTS OF MADRID. EARLY AFTERNOON

The population mainly comprises families of workers. Migrants from the south, from Extremadura or La Mancha.

Leo drives down one of the streets in the area and parks her car opposite a block of flats. She gets out of her car with the two plastic bags, and rings the bell to the fourth floor. A voice replies:

                              VOICE
Who is it?

                               LEO
It's me . . . Leo.

> *Cries of delight can be heard from inside. The entryphone clicks. Leo pushes against the door. She has her hands full with the bags of clothing.*

INT. THE BUILDING WHERE ROSA LIVES. A LANDING. AFTERNOON

The building has no lift. By the time Leo reaches the third floor she is starting to look rather tired. Before she reaches the fourth floor, Rosa opens the door and steps outside. She finds her sister on the landing and shouts 'Leo!'

Rosa walks down the steps to Leo. They kiss. Rosa helps her with the bags. As they walk upstairs to her flat, Rosa talks and looks inside the bags. Both sisters are very pleased to see each other. Both are also exhausted.

                    ROSA
What have you brought us?

                    LEO
A few clothes.

                    ROSA
Why did you bother?

                    LEO
If you don't like something or it's no use, just tell me . . .

                    ROSA
Of course it'll be useful! What I can't wear, my little girl will. It all
looks so new, Leo!

   They reach the door, which is open.

INT. ROSA'S PLACE. AFTERNOON

*When they both reach the door left open by Rosa, their mother appears.
A woman in her mid-sixties, wearing her hair flattened against her skull
and tied up in a wispy bun, she wears dark glasses even inside, and an
old dressing-gown that's been much mended, and an even more
threadbare, matching apron.*

                    MOTHER
              (*kissing her daughter, euphoric*)
My little girl! My little girl's come!

                    LEO
How are you, mum?

                    MOTHER
Quite rough. What do you expect!

   *Creating a fair racket, the three women walk across the tiny hallway
   and into the small lounge, dominated by a rectangular glass table, a
   large sideboard complete with television, and a semi-circular sofa.*

   *A very narrow passageway leads off from the lounge. On the opposite
   side, a French window hints at a small terrace. All in all, a space that
   is modest, clean and tasteless.*

LEO
How come?

ROSA
She's been depressed for days.

LEO
It's the weather . . . and Madrid!

As the three of them sit around the glass table

ROSA
The weather? It's her nerves really! She gets worked up over nothing!

MOTHER
(*aggressive*)
Shut up, you ferret-face!
(*to Leo*)
As far as your sister's concerned, it's all nerves and figments of my imagination!

Rosa is slightly younger than Leo, dressed like a typical housewife in a poor area. She is the wife of an out of work engineering worker with arty aspirations. Some of her husband's 'personal' creations are around the house. All very ugly. The women's relationship is entirely spontaneous and warm, though they see little of each other. Their different social status is of no importance whatsoever. Rosa's face wears the mask of the resigned victim, a woman used to picking up the pieces.

Leo tries to prevent a confrontation between mother and sister.

LEO
Don't argue. It must be the weather . . . I feel just the same . . .

MOTHER
My legs are like lead balloons.

LEO
Mum, you should get out . . . go for walks. You'll go to seed in here . . .

37

MOTHER

I have gone to seed.

LEO
(*to Rosa*)

Why don't you take her out?

ROSA
(*protesting*)

She's the one who doesn't want to go out.

They've sat down around the tables in the diner-lounge. Daylight comes in via the window, filtered through creamy net curtains.

The mother speaks firmly; her aggressive, stubborn manner is not without spontaneous charm.

MOTHER

Why should I go out? So I can get killed by a skinhead or knocked down by a car?
(*to Leo*)
Tell me, what did I ever do to those skinheads, you can't imagine the looks they give me . . .!

ROSA
(*to Leo*)

Getting blinder by the day . . . And she refuses to go to the optician's!

Leo takes a book out, the Amanda Gris *Anthology, from the True Love series, published by Fascination Books. The same book Angel suggested she wrote five pages on.*

LEO

Well, I've brought you the latest Amanda Gris. The first edition has sold out.

MOTHER
(*complaining*)

Look, love, I can't read novels or knit anymore.
(*almost whimpering*)
I spend the whole day with my arms crossed. The fact is I can't see a thing.

Leo leaves the book on the table.

38

ROSA

The optician told me that if she'd agree to an operation she'd more or less get her sight back . . .

MOTHER
(*to Leo*)
You sister's main aim in life is to get me on the operating table.
(*to Rosa*)
I don't want an operation! While I'm alive you won't get me on any operating table. When I die, you can do what you want with my body.

LEO
Mum, for God's sake!

MOTHER
But don't worry, there won't be much for you to get your teeth into.

Rosa shakes her head impatiently.

ROSA
(*to Leo*)
Look how she gets, just because she's told to go to the optician.

MOTHER
What can he tell me?

ROSA
What can he tell you, for heaven's sake? He's a doctor.

MOTHER
Well, he's never been right about me so far.
(*to Leo*)
Leo, an operation is like an uncut melon, till you open it you don't know if it's good or gone off . . .

Leo smiles at the comparison. Looking kindly, mother suddenly gets up in a hurry.

MOTHER
(*to Leo*)
I'm off to the lavatory. I'm so constipated . . . if I don't use a glycerine suppository I can't shit.

All of Amanda Gris's novels are carefully arranged on one of the shelves of the cocktail bar. Several dozen. Rosa places the anthology next to the other novels. On the wall are photos, both the son and daughters' first communions. The mother leaves the two sisters by themselves.

INT. ROSA'S HOUSE. LATE AFTERNOON

Sadly, Leo watches her walking off down the narrow passage. She finds it hard experiencing the rapid deterioration in her mother. Rosa, however, is used to it, for her it's quite natural. If she complains, she does so quite unmelodramatically about something that's become part and parcel of life.

ROSA

She's no patience. She'd like to be shitting all the time, that's why she uses a suppository a day.

She shakes her head helplessly; suddenly, she changes expression, as if she's just remembered something.

Hey, I've not offered you anything, my poor head . . .! I've made you something to eat.

Leo gets up, and follows her into the tiny kitchen, if only to keep her company.

LEO

I'll just have a coffee, I told you not to cook anything.

INT. ROSA'S KITCHEN. AFTERNOON

The narrow kitchen looks on to a glass-enclosed space for drying clothes and storage.

ROSA
(preparing the coffee)

I can't argue back, she goes for you. You don't know how aggressive she gets!

LEO

She's bored . . . used to village life . . . She's stifled here.

ROSA

She's getting like her sister Petra.

LEO

Don't say that. Aunt Petra was mad at birth. Mum's manias are to do with growing old . . .

ROSA

What about her aunts, and her grandma? They all went mad . . . Mum's got it in her blood.
(*changing her tone*)
I've cooked these squid 'just the way you like them'.

LEO

No . . . no . . . Thank you.
(*changes her tone*)
I'd like you to tell me how we'll end up. We've got the same blood as her.

Rosa prefers to ignore her sister's remarks.

ROSA
(*taking no notice*)
Have you noticed how she's dressed? She looks like a bag-lady. Some crème caramel? Made from just milk and eggs! You won't say no to that!

She shows her a crème caramel that fills the whole of one big plate. It looks mouth-watering.

LEO

Just a small piece.

Leo serves herself a small piece. Licks her lips. Both sit next to one of the table-tops alongside the kitchen wall.

Oh, I've brought you something.
(*hands over money in an envelope*).
Here you are.

Rosa takes it, reluctantly.

ROSA

I'll take it for the time being, till Santiago finds some work.

41

LEO

How is he?

ROSA

Not very good . . . doing odd jobs . . . and drinking more by the
day. With Mum there, calling him a drunkard to his face . . . And
me in the firing line.

Rosa gets up. Takes the coffee off the hob.

LEO
(*sounding quite unsure of herself*)
Perhaps I should take her with me.

ROSA

How on earth can you take her with you!

LEO

It's no life for you.

ROSA

I'm used to it now.

*She opens the small cupboard just above her head to get cups out.
Their mother appears in the doorway to the hall.*

INT. ROSA'S KITCHEN. AFTERNOON

Mother bursts into the kitchen shouting.

MOTHER

Are you criticising me?

ROSA

What a fright you gave me! I almost broke the cups!

Mother goes into the tiny kitchen.

MOTHER
(*to Leo*)
Don't take any notice of her, Leo. I'm still quite with it . . .
(*gestures as if in pain*)
If only my feet felt as well as my head. My pins are in a right state
. . . I can't depend on them.

ROSA

You shouldn't eat so much salty stuff. Your blood pressure's gone
wild . . .

MOTHER

And you're the real cross I have to bear!

LEO

Stop arguing right now! Mum, why don't you wear the dressing-
gown I gave you?

MOTHER

It's very beautiful, and should be in a museum.

LEO

I bought it for you to wear.

MOTHER

It's much better put away . . .

ROSA

Just like a bag-lady. I'm ashamed to be seen in the street with her.

It's true, her mother's garb couldn't be more threadbare or patched.

MOTHER
(*protests to Leo*)

I can't do anything to please your sister. She's as touchy as my
sister Petra, may she rest in peace . . . A chip off the same
block . . .

*The mother goes to the back of the room: where the refrigerator,
cupboards and shelves are set against the narrow kitchen wall.*

ROSA

You've certainly turned out like your sister and aunts! And your
grandma!

MOTHER

And who else?

LEO

Please, leave our genes in peace!

Mother looks for something by the refrigerator.

43

MOTHER
(*to Leo*)

One of these days I'll clear off back to the village! Then I won't be in anyone's way! Ay, my love, it's so sad!

Her lament refers to old age, in the abstract, and, in particular, to her own . . .

ROSA
(*upset*)

Who said you were in the way?

MOTHER

After meals, I doze off a bit . . . and she wakes me up, like a sergeant-major.

ROSA

Otherwise she can't get to sleep at night.

MOTHER

Stir yourself . . . Stir yourself . . . Heavens! What do you expect me to do, aerobics? Perhaps I'll die soon and then I won't bother anyone!
(*shouting*)

Where've you put them . . .? She hides everything away like a magpie!

ROSA
(*screaming*)

What are you after?!

Her mother responds in kind, at the top of her voice.

MOTHER

The baked peppers!

Rosa points to the corner, right by her mother.

ROSA

The baked peppers are there!

MOTHER
(*to Leo*)

Didn't I tell you? I'm as blind as a bat!

The mother looks for a plastic bag in which she can put the glass jar containing the baked peppers.

ROSA

Blind she may be, but she still wants to go back to the village. And can't even wait for the school holidays . . .

MOTHER

I don't want to be in Madrid!

LEO
(*conciliatory*)

Mum, you can't live by yourself in the village. We have to find a woman to look after the house and keep you company at night.

MOTHER

I bet. Who'll poke around my cupboards and eat my black puddings. No chance!

ROSA

You just can't get through to her!

The mother wraps the jar of peppers in a plastic bag.

LEO

Mum, the village is much healthier for you. But you can't live alone anymore!

Their mother takes no notice of her and changes tone; she's got the move from anger to tenderness and vice versa down to a fine art.

MOTHER

Here you are. I've cooked these peppers for you. They're inside the bag.

Leo takes the jar of peppers from her mother.

LEO

Why do you bother? I've got a cook.

MOTHER

I'd like to taste that gypsy's cooking!

ROSA

What a racist!

LEO

It's great! And you can't imagine her ironing! Paco says nobody
irons shirts like her. Not even me.

MOTHER
(*interrupting*)
Well, I don't think he'll be as well looked after at war as he is at
home.

*Rosa listens. It's the only time she looks in agreement with her mother
and doesn't contradict her. She backs her up by keeping quiet.*

Leo's expression changes, but she doesn't say anything either.

I can see you're in a real state, Leo. Going off to war.
(*looks at Rosa, who's nodding*)
As if we didn't have enough headaches.

By keeping silent Leo seems to be agreeing with her mother.

Every day I pray for him . . . that nothing happens to him.

LEO

Pray for me as well.

MOTHER

Of course, my love, you first.

ROSA

But you never pray for me.

MOTHER

You're an atheist.

ROSA

What do you care. Pray! Out of the way or you'll get hit!

*Rosa looks for a plastic container in the cupboards above her mother's
head.*

MOTHER
(*to Leo*)
Hey, while we're about it. You've got to give me a hand to pay the
rates in the village.

Leo takes out another envelope and gives it to her.

LEO

I haven't forgotten . . . here you are.

ROSA

More crème caramel?

LEO

No.

ROSA

I'll put it in the Tupperware and you can take it with you . . . I'll put the squid in another one.

MOTHER

Don't forget it's the boy's birthday next week.

ROSA

For God's sake, Mum! Stop asking! The boy wants for nothing.

MOTHER

He could do with some jeans, he's always wearing the same pair. He's quite a little man now! You don't know how well-behaved and studious he's turned out . . . not like his crazy sister . . . who can't even wash her knickers.

ROSA

They're the same age. Grandmother and granddaughter.
(*to Leo*)
Here's your crème caramel.

She bangs the Tupperware on the table. The mother counts the money inside the envelope Leo gave her.

MOTHER
(*still counting*)
Leocadia! What a cross I have to bear!

She's referring to Rosa.

Leo is reading She Imagines *by Juan José Millas. While drinking a whisky, she underlines the text: 'And he explained that* anís *drinkers and consumers of marijuana often feel like they're robots. Seeing oneself as a robot is typical of individuals whose capacity for suffering has been overwhelmed by some awful event.'*

We hear her in voice-over, see it in the book, and see her underlining the words in pencil, very close-up. When she says anís *drinkers, Leo questions (or corrects) the text and adds 'whisky'.*

The telephone rings. Leo abandons Millás's book, gulps down some whisky, and picks up the mobile phone that's on her desk. She thinks it's her husband ringing her.

ANGEL

Hello, it's Angel.

LEO

What Angel?

ANGEL

Angel. From *El País*. I'm sorry but I couldn't wait till tomorrow. I've read both the essays and your novel . . . and I thought they were wonderful.

LEO
(*incredulous*)

You mean you liked them?

ANGEL

Very much so.

LEO

Sure you're not pulling my leg?

Leo has another drink.

ANGEL

As if I . . .?

LEO

Have you been drinking?
                    (*downing some more whisky*)

48

ANGEL

Yes, and when I drink I don't lie. In other words, get yourself a pseudonym, because I want to print 'The Pain of Living' in the next supplement. Do you mind if I get friendly and call you 'tú'?

LEO

No please 'tú' me as much as you want to.

ANGEL

I just love the title . . . 'The Pain of Living'.

LEO

It's a line from a song by Bola de Nieve.

ANGEL

I know the one. 'If all I have is the pain of living. Oh, love! Don't let me live.' Nobody would ever have thought of linking that Cuban feeling with Djuna Barnes, yet they've a lot in common.

LEO

Yes, exactly what I wanted to bring out.

ANGEL

On that, have you got a publisher for the novel? I could help you.

LEO
(*surprised*)

Well . . . the truth is . . . I wasn't thinking of publishing it.

ANGEL

So, why did you write it?

LEO
(*hesitating*)

I felt like it . . . I like writing . . . I told you.

ANGEL

Fine, come in and talk to me about work. And I'm sorry about yesterday . . . I'm not a jerk . . . but sometimes I act quite idiotically.

They hang up.

INT. AT HER WORK-TABLE. NIGHT

Leo stares at the telephone, pleased with herself. She needs to share the good news with somebody. She looks at her wristwatch, it's not very late, almost midnight. She has another drink, to gather strength, and dials her husband's number in Brussels. A sleepy voice responds at the other end of the line.

                              LEO
Paco . . . it's me.

                              PACO
                        (*voice-over*)
What time is it, Leo?

                              LEO
Early.

                              PACO
                  (*voice-over, protesting*)
It's almost twelve o'clock! I was asleep. Is something the matter?

                              LEO
                        (*hesitantly*)
Yes. I'm very happy and I wanted to share it with you . . . I went
to look for work at *El País*.

                              PACO
                        (*voice-over*)
You've been drinking?

                              LEO
No. Why?

   Leo looks at her glass reproachfully.

                              PACO
                        (*voice-over*)
You sound very lively for this time of night.

   Leo has lost interest. Paco's reaction depresses her.

                              LEO
                        (*damp-eyed*)
It's not late for Madrid . . .

PACO
(*voice-over*)
It's never late in Madrid, but this is Brussels.

LEO
(*disappointed*)
All right, I'll phone you tomorrow . . . and tell you . . .

PACO
(*voice-over, he notices her change of tone*)
Are you OK?

LEO
Yes, I'm fine, love . . .
(*half-relaxing*)
Lots of kisses. Till tomorrow. Tomorrow all will be revealed.

PACO
(*voice-over, awkward*)
If you think it's that important . . .
(*yawning loudly*)

LEO
(*depressed*)
No, love, it can wait. Sorry I woke you up.

PACO
(*voice-over*)
Good night.

Leo hangs up, looking serious and down-in-the-mouth.

INT. AT HER WORK-TABLE. DAY

Ellipsis.

The telephone is in the same place as the previous night, on Leo's desk. But now it's the following morning. Leo dials the Brussels number again. She says very little – and in French.

LEO
Est-ce que je peux parler avec Monsieur le Lieutenant-Colonel Francisco Arcos?

A BELGIAN
(*voice-over*)
Il ne se trouve pas. Qui est-ce qui l'appelle?

LEO

Sa femme, de Madrid. Dis-lui que je l'ai appelé, et de m'appeler, s'il vous plaît.

  Leo hangs up, this time very annoyed.

EXT. THE WAREHOUSE OF FASCINATION BOOKS. DAY

A factory area, reminiscent of the Tribeca district in New York. Garages and warehouses, an atmosphere of industrial decline. A delivery lorry, open at the back, is unloading its merchandise on the pavement outside the entrance to Fascination Books. Inside is an enormous warehouse full of books.

A fork-lift truck inserts its metal shafts into the back of the vehicle and takes out a pallet with several layers of books. On the other side of the street large groups of women workers keep walking by from Induico, a subsidiary of the Corte Inglés. They're in uniform, although because of the cold and each individual's character, the uniformity is undermined by other garments they wear. Tired, their hair in a mess and their make-up even worse, the group of women workers walk by the vehicle, in the style of Lang's Metropolis. *Woman as slave. (A metaphor in light-blue overalls for Leo herself, doubly chained, as we shall see later.)*

The pallet of books reaches ground level. Leo approaches along the pavement from the far side. By the entrance Alicia is signalling to the driver of the lorry. She sees Leo and says hello. (Alicia is an irritable woman, in her forties. She could be production manager, secretary, housekeeper or a housewife.)

ALICIA

Well! Well! Leo . . . at last!

INT. THE WAREHOUSE OF FASCINATION BOOKS. DAY

Leo greets the woman. The fork-lift truck deposits the pallet of books in the entrance to the warehouse. The two women walk in. Alicia picks a copy off the top layer. She half shows it to Leo, presumably Leo recognizes the volume. It's Amanda Gris's Anthology. *The same volume Angel was recommending her at* El País.

ALICIA

Look, into a second edition already!

Leo nods.

I thought you'd never come . . .

LEO

I've been busy . . .

They start walking between towers of variegated books. Some of them reach the ceiling. Apart from being the offices of the Fascination series, the place acts as a warehouse for books that are about to be distributed. They handle every kind of publication, text-book, recent novels, etc. These are carefully packed on rows of shelves that in turn create streets; the inside of the warehouse is like a small underground city, with tall skyscrapers of books or piles of cardboard boxes. Leo and Alicia walk along its narrow avenues till they reach the latter's office. The atmosphere is Kafkaesque par excellence.

Leo is still by the door that looks on to the street.

LEO

Did you get the novel? I sent it last week.

ALICIA
(*gravely*)

Yes, naturally, we received it.

LEO

And?

ALICIA

Leo, that wasn't an Amanda Gris novel you sent us. Why this change?

They're alone. Nobody can hear them. After Angel's praise, Leo was expecting a more positive reaction from Alicia. Although the audience doesn't know this yet, they're talking about the same novel.

LEO

I suppose I'm maturing.

53

ALICIA

Why?

LEO
(*interrupting her, ironically*)
Perhaps because I'm alive . . .

ALICIA
I mean . . . why change, if sales are still up?
(*She doesn't give* LEO *time to reply*)
Leo, you're forgetting our series is called *True Love*. How could
you send us a story about a mother who finds out her daughter has
killed her father after he's tried to rape her? And so nobody can
find out, the mother puts him to hibernate in the cold store
belonging to a neighbour's restaurant?

LEO
Getting rid of a corpse isn't easy and for the mother saving her
daughter is really important. Wouldn't you do what you could to
save your daughter?

INT. ALICIA'S OFFICE. THE BUSINESS COMPLEX OF FASCINATION
BOOKS. DAY.

*They reach the door to Alicia's office. They go in. The office is suitably
plain and sordid. There are posters on the walls, in particular of some
novels by Amanda Gris. The illustrations are dominated by the aesthetic
of the photo-novelette. (Use 'Jazmín' as a reference point) Apart from
two big work tables, there's also a sidetable, a coffee-maker and
minibar, and books everywhere. The top part of the walls is made of
glass, so we can see most of the warehouse: the city of paper.*

*Alicia fleetingly greets Tomás, a grey, sinister-looking man who's a
complete alcoholic. Alicia goes over to her desk, followed by Leo. Tomás
pours himself a drink in one corner and looks at them. One of the three
then lights a pipe, filling the room with clouds of smoke.*

ALICIA
(pouring herself a drink)
We're not talking daughters but novels. Children exist to steal
our lives from us, and novels to give us the illusion we're still
living them. When someone buys one of our novels they want to
forget their sordid existence . . . to dream of a better life even
though it's a lie. Who wants to dream of people living in down-
at-heel districts, unemployed, the left-overs, genuine death-
warmed-up?

She picks up from her desk-top a copy of The Cold Store *identical to
the one Leo took Angel in his office at* El País.

Who can identify with a protagonist busy cleaning shit off patients
in a hospital, with a junkie mother-in-law and a queer son who's
into blacks?

She puts The Cold Store *back on the table.*

Are you out of your mind, Leo?

LEO
Perhaps I am, Alicia, but that's real life.

ALICIA
Reality! We've all got enough reality at home. Reality is for the
newspapers and television. And look at the results. Seeing and

reading so much reality is why the country's about to blow up. Reality should be banned!

TOMÁS

Keep your hair on, Alicia. It's nobody's fault your son's a junkie.

ALICIA
(to Tomás)

That's none of your business!
(to Leo)

On that subject, is it true you gave my son five thousand pesetas the other day?

LEO

Did I . . .? But I don't know him.

ALICIA

Well, he knows you. Or says he does, from seeing you around here. I suppose he must have stolen them from me . . .
(she explains)

It's incredible! He swore to me that he met you in the street and that you gave them to him for helping to take your boots off. So inventive! He'll drive me mad!

LEO

That was your son? Then it's true I did give him the money . . .

ALICIA

Really? The story was so ridiculous . . . I almost believed him.

At the mention of her son, Alicia gets stirred up. The two women fall silent for a moment, then Tomás interrupts.

TOMÁS

Let's concentrate . . . If we start talking about drugs, we'll never get to the point.

ALICIA
(dreamily)

That's right.

TOMÁS

Leo, we contracted you to write love stories.

Leo makes no attempt to persuade him; or even defend herself.

LEO

There's a terrific love story in the novel.

Alicia picks up the thread of the conversation, still rather distracted.

ALICIA

Which one? Not on the pages I read.

LEO
(in a depressed, sober tone)

The restaurant owner, the one who can't forget his wife, although he's separated from her . . .

ALICIA
(scandalized, incredulous, with renewed energy)

The one who decides to hire a killer to finish off his mother-in-law, because he's sure his wife will go to the funeral, and that way he'll see her, talk to her and persuade her to come back to him!!?

LEO

That's him.

ALICIA

Do you think the best way to track down a woman is by killing her mother?

LEO

You won't believe me but I based it on a real event. It happened in Puerto Rico.

ALICIA

You're having me on.

LEO
(downcast)

No. I'm sorry you didn't like the novel.

She gets up as if to leave the office. Tomás's voice stops her.

TOMÁS

Wait a minute. We have got a problem, Leo.

Leo stands and stares at him unmoved.

TOMÁS

You're contracted to us to deliver five love stories a year for the next three years.

He reads out a clause in the contract.

Novels about romance and the jet-set, in cosmopolitan settings . . . suggestive sex that's never more than a suggestion . . . winter sports, sunny skies, residential areas, undersecretaries, ministers, yuppies . . . No politics . . . No social conscience . . . but illegitimate children are fine . . . Happy endings, etc.

He reads from a copy of the contract.

Leo, standing up, looks at him impassively.

ALICIA

The contract also specifies the millions you'll receive as an advance. And your conditions
                    (irritated tone of voice)
that we can't use your real name or ever reveal it, or give out any photos of you, no interviews. We swallowed all that and till now have kept to the letter.

TOMÁS

But you haven't. And there's the rub.

Tomás's words couldn't be clearer or colder. Leo's still standing, on the point of leaving. First, she explains herself.

LEO

It's a colour problem.

TOMÁS

Leo, play it straight, don't get clever-clever with me!

LEO

I can't write a rose-tinted novel, it comes out black. I try, but each page comes out blacker than black.

ALICIA

Absurd! You've been writing love stories for twenty years . . .! You can't lose that overnight.

LEO

The whole world can change overnight. I'm going.

ALICIA

Will you have another try before Tomás sues you for breach of
contract? Think of your holiday home, your independence, your
trips to the Caribbean, your collagen, your liposuctions, your poor
family, your anonymity.

LEO
(*depressed*)

Goodbye, Alicia!

She walks over to the door.

TOMÁS
(*threatening her*)

Don't try to two-time us, Leo.

LEO

Two-time? I only wanted to be frank with you, though that's not
in the contract.

TOMÁS

Talk to your lawyer . . . he'll tell you what you're risking.

Leo leaves. Alicia shouts after her.

ALICIA

Leo, don't go like that! If Tomás sues you, everyone will find out
you're Amanda Gris . . .!
(*to herself*)
Though really it wouldn't be bad publicity for a second anthology.
A hell of a story . . . finding out who she is, who's she's married
to . . .
(*looks at Tomás, her mind made up*)
You must sue her, Tomás!

*Leo disappears round a corner in the warehouse, engulfed by the
jungle of paper.*

*In the doorway, Leo walks by a pallet full of books written by her.
Her first anthology. The sequence finishes on a close-up of her books.
Over this image someone can be heard violently attacking a*

*typewriter keyboard. The machine and the violence both belong to
Leo.*

INT. LEO'S HOUSE. STUDY. AFTERNOON

*Leo's voice-over can be heard above the crash of the keyboard, reading
the contents of her angry text.*

*Leo's sitting in front of her typewriter, at her desk, bathed in the light of
a Madrid afternoon. Next to the typewriter, a glass of whisky rises up
out of the mess on the table, eternally partnered by a steaming ashtray.
Leo entitles her essay 'An Anthology of Absences'.*

LEO
(voice-over)

The only quality I recognize in Amanda Gris is that she hid in
the shadow of a pseudonym and didn't show her face in the past
twenty years of her hegemony over the bookstalls. In times like
these, her lack of self-advertisement is perhaps worthy of
admiration. But we know little of her literary technique. I don't
know whether she handwrites or types. Truman Capote
differentiated between writers and typists. We don't even know
whether Amanda Gris is a good typist. Hers is pure fiction, but
nobody should think that it bears any relation to literary creation.
When I say 'fiction' I mean 'deceit'. Amanda Gris is no
writer . . .

INT. ANGEL'S OFFICE. MID-AFTERNOON

*The text Leo's writing appears on the fax in Angel's office. Angel picks
it up and starts reading, impressed by Leo's aggression.*

ANGEL
(exclaims to himself)

Amazing!

EXT. CALLE JOSÉ ABASCAL. MID-AFTERNOON

*Leo walks past an enormous window display for Rock bathroom
furniture. It's like a stage-set. Some six metres long, the window shows,
in an angled shot (so it's quite visible), a complete bathroom in finest
detail. The impact is theatrical and rather eerie. Leo stares at a Red*

Cross-shaped medicine cupboard. She's got an identical one, in her bathroom.

There's an ominous whiff in the air. Across the bottom of the window, stuck on like a transfer, is the firm's slogan: 'I love you. ♥! Rock.'

After looking at it, Leo disappears in the direction of the entrance next door: the house where Betty lives.

EXT. BETTY'S HOUSE. STREET. MID-AFTERNOON

Betty lives in the building next door to the bathroom shop. Leo presses the entryphone bell. She's wearing the same clothes that she wore to Fascination Books. Presumably, she finished the critical article and then rushed to her friend's house. She presses the bell again. Betty responds.

> BETTY
> *(voice-over)*

Who's that?

> LEO

It's Leo. Will you let me in?

> BETTY
> *(voice-over, lying)*

Leo, I was just going . . . Why didn't you telephone before?

> LEO

I did, but you were engaged.

> BETTY
> *(voice-over)*

Couldn't you have waited?

> LEO
> *(cross)*

No, but if you're going to keep me out here on the pavement, I'll leave . . .

The entryphone clicks. In a temper, Leo pushes the door open.

INT. BETTY'S HOUSE. MID-AFTERNOON

Leo reaches her girl-friend's flat. Betty has already opened the door. She

doesn't look as if she's ready to go out yet, and is smoking nervously.
Leo is as bad tempered as she was at the end of the previous sequence.

LEO
(*irritable*)
Betty, I wouldn't have bothered you, but I've got a really serious
problem and wanted your advice.

BETTY
(*equally irritable*)
I've got problems of my own . . . Perhaps we should swap them,
like pin-ups . . .

*Betty, quite unawares, looks anxiously at her watch. Leo is really
furious and reproachful.*

LEO
(*leaving*)
Thanks very much. I'm sorry, I thought you were a friend of mine.

Betty follows Leo.

BETTY
If I'm your friend, why don't you ask what's the matter with me?

*Leo turns round to Betty. The argument continues. Evidently she
didn't intend leaving.*

LEO
You didn't give me time! I came to see you because you are the
only person I can talk to about Amanda Gris. But now you
mention it . . . you do seem very strange, Betty . . . What's
wrong?

*In a normal tone of voice, as if she's just realized. She no longer feels
insulted.*

BETTY
I can't tell you.

LEO
(*positively*)
Really?

BETTY

Professional problems.

LEO

We are in a state! Let's go for a drink.

It's an absurd situation, but it calms Leo down, she's used to absurdity. The telephone rings. Betty stops opposite Leo for a few seconds, until Leo is forced to tell her.

The phone's ringing.

BETTY

Are you sure?

The telephone's still ringing.

LEO

Yes, it's the telephone. Can't you hear it?

BETTY
(*rather confused*)

Yes, of course . . . but I'll get you a drink.

LEO

Shall I pick it up?

BETTY
(*suddenly*)

No . . .! No . . .! I will!

Betty runs to the phone, under the amused, astonished gaze of Leo, who mutters to herself.

LEO

She's worse than I am.

INT. CONTINUED. BETTY'S HOUSE. MID-AFTERNOON

Betty picks up the nearest phone. When she hears the voice at the other end of the line, her expression changes. She draws on all her talents to hide her annoyance.

Leo stands, as if adrift in the hallway, speechless, a reluctant listener to Betty's telephone conversation.

BETTY

Heavens! What a surprise . . .! That's right . . . she's just arrived . . . Here she is . . .

Leo guesses they're referring to her.

Leo, it's for you.

LEO
(taken aback)

For me? Who is it?

BETTY

Here you are!

Leo picks up the phone. She also changes her tone radically. Nobody would know she'd been arguing a moment earlier.

LEO

Who is it . . .? Paco! What a surprise! How did you know I was here?

Leo is happy rather than surprised.

PACO
(voice-over)

I called home, and as you weren't in, I thought perhaps you'd gone to see Betty.

LEO
(pleased and flattered at his interest)

Wow, that was really telepathic, I've not been here for weeks.

PACO
(voice-over)

As you're always saying, if I don't find you at home, I should persevere and comb the whole city for you!

LEO

I like it!

PACO
(voice-over)

Did you go to see her for anything in particular?

LEO

Yes . . . I'll tell you . . . I've got myself in a fix . . . But tell me first
if there are any rocks round there?

PACO
(*voice-over*)

Of course, there are.

LEO

Lots of rocks? It's like the Grand Canyon here . . .

PACO
(*voice-over*)

Hey, what's wrong?

LEO

I've split with Fascination. I can't tell you the details because it's
very complicated and I don't expect you've got the time . . .

*Leo's comment is clearly ironical. Betty goes over to a kind of cocktail
bar. Takes two glasses of whisky. One for her and the one for Leo.
Gives it to her at an opportune moment.*

PACO
(*voice-over*)

It's true, I haven't got much time. But in three days' time you can
tell me everything in person.

LEO
(*almost shouting*)

What? Did I hear right?

PACO
(*voice-over*)

Yes. I've finally managed a day's leave.

*Passionate, her eyes watering, Leo displays her emotions, not in the
least self-conscious. Betty looks at her, impressed by her friend's
spontaneity.*

LEO

Really? You can't imagine how I'm longing to see you! It'll all turn
out fine this time, I swear . . . not like my trip to Brussels.

She cries, relieved.

>   PACO
>   *(voice-over)*

I hope so.

>   LEO
>   *(tearful)*

Really . . .

>   *(sincerely)*

I promise.

>   PACO
>   *(voice-over)*

But don't cry . . .

>   LEO

It's emotional. Tears of happiness
>   *(sounds happy)*
. . . there we are. No more tears. Feel that self-control?

>   PACO
>   *(voice-over)*

Good. Give my best wishes to Betty.

>   LEO
>   *(relaying)*

Best wishes from Paco.

>   BETTY
>   *(serious)*

Best wishes from me too.

>   LEO

She sends her best wishes too.

>   PACO
>   *(voice-over)*

How is she?

>   LEO

Got her problems, the poor dear.

PACO
(*voice-over*)

Such as?

LEO

I don't know . . . She can't tell me
(*to Betty*)
What's wrong?

BETTY

I'm fed up!

LEO
(*repeats*)
She's fed up! . . . Are you? Really? . . . Yes, of course . . .

PACO
(*voice-over*)
All right, dear. I must leave you. Lots of kisses.

LEO

To you as well, my darling. Lots of rocks.

And hangs up, ecstatic.

INT. BETTY'S HOUSE. MID-AFTERNOON

Betty's putting on make-up in the presence of Leo, right in the middle of the lounge. There's a bag of creams, make-up, false eye-lashes etc. open on the table. Leo's beside herself. The conversation with Paco has removed the sour taste left by the day up till then.

However, Betty's strange irritability lingers on, slightly softened by the disruption.

BETTY

How peculiar that Paco rang here.

LEO
(*making a show of it*)
He didn't find me at home, and as he knows you're the only person I ever see . . .

67

BETTY

Is he coming?

LEO

Yes. In three days . . .

BETTY

Well, see if you can sort out your situation once and for all. Try not to shout, listen to him, let him talk . . . Don't whine . . . Act like an adult.

LEO

There'll be no fights this time, I swear!

BETTY

Hey, what's all this about rocks? You asked Paco if there were any rocks in Brussels.

LEO
(*smiling*)

Oh, it's our way of saying 'I love you' without anyone else understanding.
(*explains*)

Years ago . . . just after we were married . . . We saw an advert for Rock toiletware . . . You've got one right next door . . .

BETTY

Yes. They've recently opened the shop . . .

Betty looks at her, upset and intrigued.

LEO

The slogan said 'I love you. Rock.' I don't know if you noticed . . . When we speak on the phone to each other in front of people who we don't want to find out, saying rock or lots of rock to each other is our way of saying we're very much in love.

Betty doesn't know how to react. She doesn't, but looks rather pensive, ruminating over her own worries.

INT. LEO'S ROOM

The following morning.

Leo is searching frantically on the side-dresser among the jewels in a shell-encrusted case she uses as a jewellery box. Evidently, she can't find what she's looking for. She can hear Blanca's footsteps coming along the passage towards her bedroom.

When Blanca appears in the doorway, Leo gives her a look of frustration and anguish. Blanca tries to cheer her up by showing her a knitted garment she's carrying, a sweater wrapped in a plastic bag. She's also carrying a copy of El País, *which she puts down on the bed.*

BLANCA
(*triumphantly*)
It was at the dry-cleaner's! The girl told me you left it there a week ago.

LEO
Well, I'd forgotten.
(*sorrowfully*)
I don't feel well, Blanca. And now I can't find my onyx earrings either, I wanted to wear them this morning.

Leo is about to burst into tears, she's so on edge. Blanca looks worried as well.

BLANCA
I don't like jewels to go missing. Not one bit . . .! I'm the only person who comes in here.

The telephone rings. Leo looks for the portable phone, but can't find that either.

LEO
(*distressed*)
Where can I have left the phone?

She goes round the house, from bedroom to lounge, followed by Blanca. Neither finds the phone. A voice erupts from the answer-machine.

ANGEL
(*voice-over*)
Leo? It's Angel. Are you coming in this morning . . .? Could you please confirm . . .

(he pauses)

Listen, I've just read an interview we're printing next weekend, Bigas Luna is preparing a film with a plot that is very similar, too similar I'd say, to your 'Cold Store' . . .

Leo presses the button that allows her to speak without picking up the receiver.

LEO

It's me, Angel . . .

INT. ANGEL'S OFFICE. DAY

Angel taps the A4 sheets on the table in front of him which contain the interview he's referring to.

This conversation alternates between Angel's office and Leo's lounge.

ANGEL

What's wrong?

LEO

Nothing . . .

ANGEL

You sound strange.

LEO

That's because I'm talking with no hands.

ANGEL

Hey, do you know a scriptwriter called Juan José Burés?

LEO

Doesn't ring a bell.

ANGEL

Well he's written a script suspiciously like your novel. Bigas Luna's going to direct it . . .

LEO

Really? What a coincidence!

ANGEL

It may not be a coincidence, but pure plagiarism.

LEO

I don't think so. You're the only person who's read my novel.

Leo knows she's lying. She thinks of Alicia and Fascination Books. They've read her novel as well, but she's not going to tell Angel that.

ANGEL

I suppose you've taken out the copyright, just in case.

LEO

No, I haven't.

ANGEL

Why not?

LEO

As I wasn't intending to publish it . . . it never occurred to me.

ANGEL

I really don't understand you, Leo. Hey, you're not the plagiarist?

Initially the question upsets her, she's about to take offence . . .

LEO

Me?

But she doesn't take offence. On the contrary, she's amused.

ANGEL

Not that I've anything against plagiarising, unless they're copying me or you.

Blanca appears at the other end of the lounge looking worried.

LEO

OK, I'll see you in a minute.

ANGEL

You didn't answer my question.

LEO
(*unapologetic*)

Well, that's true, now you mention it. I'm on my way . . .

Leo turns to where Blanca is standing.

71

BLANCA
(*contritely*)
I can't find your earrings anywhere.

EXT. THE BLOCK WHERE LEO LIVES. THE STREET

*Leo walks out. Waves down a taxi. The vehicle stops in front of her.
Leo opens the door and gets in. Apart from her handbag she's carrying
the copy of* El País *which Blanca brought her in the previous sequence.*

INT. TAXI. DAY

LEO
(*to the taxi-driver*)
Miguel Yuste, number 40.

After giving the address to the taxi-driver Leo opens El País. *She
looks for the cultural pages. To her surprise they've published two
articles on Amanda Gris. Hers and one by a certain Patchy Derm
that's totally over the top. Derm uses Amanda Gris to analyse the
upsurge in tear-jerking fiction throughout the world.*

*Leo has a pseudonym for the by-line (Paz Sufrategui). In the taxi,
she reads both articles with interest and surprise, pride and dismay.*

INT. ANGEL SERRANO'S OFFICE. DAY.

Leo walks into Angel's office, and is warmly greeted.

ANGEL
Welcome, Paz Sufrategui . . .

LEO
Shush . . .! Don't let anyone find out it's me. Thanks for
publishing my article. I was so looking forward to seeing myself in
print. On that subject, who's the other woman, the one who's all
in favour?

ANGEL
Patchy Derm?

LEO
Yes.

72

ANGEL

Yours truly.

LEO

Impossible.

ANGEL

Do you think Patchy Derm is a bit excessive? I'm only on the
flabby side, right?

LEO

Come on, Angel, writing's a very serious business, even for
Amanda Gris.

ANGEL

Well you didn't haven't much regard for her. Look tomorrow
there's a shouting competition in Colmenar de Oreja, you must
come. You've no idea.

LEO

I can't.

ANGEL

Perhaps you'd prefer a demonstration. There's a very lively
medical student demo. You could write an article about them.

LEO

I've got lots to do tomorrow. My husband's back from abroad.

ANGEL

So, there's a husband?

LEO

Yes.

ANGEL

I knew there was something separating us. An abyss between the
two of them, as Amanda Gris would put it.

*Leo gazes through the office window that overlooks an enormous floor
full of people working.*

LEO

This reminds me of *The Apartment* by Billy Wilder.

ANGEL

Me too. In that film, Shirley MacLaine fell in love with a person she thought she was in love with, but not the person she really was in love with, but someone else . . .

LEO

Look, Angel, I'm sorry but I am in love with the person I think I'm in love with.

INT. LEO'S HOME. KITCHEN

In the kitchen, Blanca's finishing preparing the ingredients for the paella. She looks very serious. She's obviously worried.

Leo walks into the kitchen. Her hair combed, dressed up, and nervy. The bell rings. Leo gives a start.

LEO

That's him! And I'm not ready yet!

BLANCA

You look great.

Blanca walks towards the door.

LEO

Do you think so?

She stops her, before she can open it.

Blanca, say hello to him, then go, OK?

BLANCA

All right . . .

LEO

And don't come back till tomorrow afternoon.

BLANCA

I've got a rehearsal in the afternoon. I told you I've got rehearsals every afternoon . . . with my son . . . who's insisted . . . I don't want to . . . but he's dug his heels in . . .

Blanca looks anxious.

74

LEO

Fine, the day after tomorrow then . . .
(*the bell rings again*)
Let me spend a whole day alone with my husband.

BLANCA

Don't you worry, madam! But I bet that's my Antonio.

LEO

I'll open up!

INT. THE HALLWAY INTO LEO'S HOME

Leo walks over and opens the door. It is Antonio. She's very disappointed.

LEO

Oh, it's you. Come in. Your mother's in the kitchen.

Leo disappears, to continue sprucing herself up.

INT. LEO'S HOUSE. KITCHEN

Antonio and Blanca in the kitchen.

ANTONIO
(*quietly so Leo can't hear him, but very tense*)
We're all waiting for you. You're the only one missing!

BLANCA
(*firmly*)
Well, carry on waiting for me! I'm working.

In a rage, Antonio knocks the kitchen top with his hand and almost fractures a finger. It's a tremendously violent scene with his mother, although they're both restraining themselves. We don't know why, but there are clearly serious problems between mother and son.

ANTONIO

For fuck's sake! Who do you think you are to keep everybody waiting?

Blanca is extremely tense, she looks at Antonio; but she's not afraid of her son's raging temper.

75

BLANCA

I told you this household comes first!

ANTONIO
(*very worked up*)
This household! Your son should come first!

BLANCA

That's right! Insult me into the bargain! Tell me I'm a bad mother!

Leo appears. She's heard the shouting, without understanding what they were saying.

LEO

What's wrong? I heard a knock.

ANTONIO
(*determined but restrained*)
Madam . . .
(*begging her*)
I want to ask you a favour . . . in exchange, ask for whatever you want.

Blanca wipes the tears away with her apron, she's crying. Leo looks at her.

LEO

Can you please tell me what's happening?

BLANCA
(*tearful*)
Don't take any notice of him, madam.

ANTONIO
(*to his mother*)
Just shut up, you!

LEO

Don't talk to your mother like that . . . !

ANTONIO
(*to Leo*)
Sorry.

76

LEO

You're making me more nervy than ever . . . I need a glass . . .
Just a drop. The day's first and last. You're both my witnesses.

She opens a kitchen cupboard and eagerly pours herself out a drink.

Antonio, do you want one?

ANTONIO

Yes, please.

Blanca looks at her son, as amazed as ever.

I've got everybody waiting in the rehearsal room . . . only my
mother's missing. An impresario's coming to see us this
afternoon. She's got to be there.

BLANCA
(reproaching him)

You've no need to mix madam up in our problems, she's got her
own to deal with.

LEO

I don't see any problem . . .
(to Antonio)
You mean you've got to take her to the studio?

ANTONIO

Yes.

LEO

What are you waiting for, Blanca?

BLANCA

But I've . . .

ANTONIO
(interrupting her)

She's shit scared. She's not danced for a long time. But she's not
backing out now . . . it's too late . . .

*Antonio glances furiously at his mother, his eyes telling her to follow
his drift.*

BLANCA

But I've . . . not finished the paella.

LEO

For God's sake, Blanca, don't worry, I'll add the final touches.

BLANCA

I don't trust . . . You're not all together at the moment . . .

ANTONIO
(*to his mother*)

Keep your nose out!

LEO

Antonio, come on, get off!
(*to Blanca*)

I just add the rice, right?

BLANCA

Yes . . .

She explains how to do it.

If you finish it before your husband arrives, put Albal silver foil over the paella dish, Don Paco likes it nice and hot . . .

LEO

Yes, he'll soon be here. All right . . . good luck.

Mother and son leave Leo alone in the kitchen. Leo cleans her lips with her fingers, and makes a promise to herself:

No more drink.

INT. LEO'S HOUSE. AFTERNOON

Ellipsis.

The door-bell rings.

Leo appears in the hall, beating her own record for speed. Looks fabulous and highly charged. She's wearing totally different clothes to the previous scene. While waiting, she's changed into a short, tight-fitting dress. She opens the door.

It's him. Her husband. Paco. Time creates a short pause while she looks

78

at her husband in the doorway, who's (almost) smiling at her, tired and bashful. He a serious, handsome man. A first-rate professional. Forty years old. A few grey hairs. Bags under his eyes. He's tired. And tense.

He enters the house and Leo's arms almost simultaneously. After a few seconds, Paco gently disengages from his wife's embrace in order to shut the door and put his suitcase on the floor. Leo embraces him again and kisses him on the mouth.

PACO

Let me shut the door.

Paco kicks it to. They kiss.

You've been drinking?

LEO

Only a drop, I swear, in the last few seconds, I've got my witnesses . . . I expected you earlier . . .

She embraces him again, rests her head on his chest.

I could stay like this for the whole of your twenty-fours' leave.

Paco strokes her head. Leo has to make an effort to hold back tears of happiness. Silence.

PACO

Is Blanca here?

Leo comes back to reality, after that eternal moment of happiness.

LEO

No. We've the house to ourselves. If you want to see Blanca you'll have to stay till the day after tomorrow.

Paco's rather disappointed by the news. Leo notices his lack of enthusiasm, the smile accompanying her reply goes cold on her.

PACO

I've brought some shirts for her to iron.

LEO

I'll iron them for you, I won't do them as well as she does, but . . .

They go into the kitchen.

79

PACO

You won't want to start ironing in the short time we've got together?

LEO
(*recovers her smile*)
My feelings entirely.

Paco notices the paella on the kitchen top, covered in kitchen foil.

PACO
Paella!

He pulls the foil back and spears the paella dish with a fork. Leo watches and waits for his verdict.

LEO
(*proudly*)
I made it . . .

Paco hints subtly at his displeasure.

Well, Blanca really made it. She did the sauce. I just added the rice . . .

Listening to herself being apologetic makes her feel humiliated.

PACO
It's cold . . .

LEO
(*bites her lip*)
I'm not.

PACO
(*didn't hear her clearly*)
What?

LEO
Nothing. If you like, I'll warm it in the micro-wave.

PACO
I don't like it re-heated.

Leo lets out five per cent of the frustration coursing through her. She glares at Paco impatiently, hungrily.

80

LEO

I'm sorry! I didn't know exactly when you'd get here, among other reasons because you didn't have the courtesy to ring and let me know.

Paco realizes he's hurt her. He softens his attitude.

PACO

I'm sorry. Don't look like that, it's OK.

Leo's eyes glint. Paco goes over and takes her hand.

LEO

Kiss me, then!

Paco kisses her on the lips. Leo puts in enough passion for both of them. The kiss has a miraculous impact. The anguish gripping her fades instantly. But her edginess remains. Hand in hand they head for the bedroom.

They go into the bedroom.

PACO

I'm going to have a shower, clean off the dirt from the journey . . . Then we must talk.

As they get near the bed in the centre of the room, compulsively Leo helps him to strip off. Paco takes off his jacket and tie.

LEO

You can't imagine all the news I've got for you.

One by one Leo undoes his shirt-buttons.

But it can wait . . .
                    (one button)
first have a shower, since that appeals so
                    (another button)
. . . then we'll fuck
                    (another button)
. . . a short rest
                    (button)
. . . then we'll fuck again
                    (button)

81

. . . and then, who knows?

She opens his shirt and smells his chest, neck and cheeks.

INT. LEO'S FLAT. THE BATHROOM

Cut straight to a close-up of the shower nozzle. Paco's underneath.

Seated on the bidet, Leo tries to speak to him. (Or standing up, leaning against the wall that separates the area of mirror, washbasin, shelf from the bath and toilet.) Leo's heart beats as loudly as the noise produced by the shower splashing against Paco's body.

Leo looks at herself in the mirror and thinks she looks ridiculous, waiting, like a hungry animal, for her husband to finish his shower, so she can sink her teeth in. When Djuna Barnes wrote 'a woman born to anxiety,' you can bet she had Leo in mind. She recognizes her hunger-for-Paco puts her in a rather humiliating situation. She also looks at his face as reflected in the mirror, through the shower curtain.

At last she hears the shower go quiet. Impatiently she grabs the towel, wraps it round his streaming body. Paco begins to rub himself dry. Leo takes another towel to help him. She can't help getting entangled with his body, rubs the towel against his nipples, kneels down and (no hands) seeks out his sex with her mouth. Improvises a wayward fellatio through the towel.

PACO

Slow down! We'll get to bed in a minute.

Leo's breathing heavily. She gets up. Rubs his hair. And rubs her body against his.

LEO

We've got a lot of catching up to do, or I'll throw myself at whoever. The phosphorous is to blame.

PACO

What phosphorous?

LEO

The pills I take for my amnesia . . . they're aphrodisiacs . . . I think. If you're away much longer, I'll turn into an erotic writer.

Paco changes his expression. He's in front of the mirror looking for and finding a deodorant. He applies it to his left arm-pit. Leo stares at him.

Paco, what's the matter?

PACO

Nothing.

Paco continues to apply the deodorant, now to his right arm-pit.

LEO

Ever since you got here I've had the feeling you're avoiding me.

PACO

Not avoiding you, but before we go to bed . . . I have something to tell you.

For a fraction of a second, Leo's heart misses a beat. Paco notices and is alarmed.

LEO
(*terrified*)

Something? What?

PACO

Calm down . . .

Leo tries to, but her eyes betray her, are disobedient. Her eyes are free agents.

LEO

I am very calm.

PACO

No, you're not calm at all.

LEO

Tell me whatever the fuck you've got to tell me!

PACO

First promise you'll be reasonable.

LEO
(*angrily*)

Who's being unreasonable?

83

You.

(*in a demanding tone*)

No shouting, no tears . . .

LEO

(*shouts*)

Who's shouting? Who's crying? Tell me!

Paco starts combing his wet hair. He monitors his wife's reactions in the mirror. Blurts it out:

PACO

I've not got a day's leave. I've got to be in Torrejón in two hours. The plane to take us to Split is waiting for me.

LEO

Two hours?

PACO

Yes. They've moved the change-over forward.

LEO

I don't believe it!

PACO

The conflict's intensified.

LEO

You can say that again!

PACO

Come on, Leo, don't be childish. I'm a soldier. I don't have to explain to you what my duty is!

LEO

(*bellowing*)

You're my husband! Do I have to explain to you what your duty is to me?

PACO

You promised me we'd park our problems till the conflict was over!

Wrapped in towels Paco walks through the door from the bathroom to the bedroom. Leo's on his heels.

Paco goes to some drawers. Takes out a clean vest and a shirt. He gets dressed, still wrangling with Leo.

> **LEO**

I'm very sorry, but I'm not made of metal. You can't just park me like a car!

> **PACO**
> (*friendlier*)

Why don't you try to understand the situation?

> **LEO**

There's nothing to understand! Between me and your work, your work comes first.

> **PACO**
> (*explains*)

I'm trying to save lots of lives!

> **LEO**
> (*pleads*)

Why not save mine?

> **PACO**

Leo! I'm talking about innocent people, people who are starving, people being killed in the bread queue, with no light, no medicine . . . no hope!

> **LEO**

You're talking about me!

> **PACO**
> (*really contemptuous*)

You're totally selfish! Can't you forget yourself just for a moment?

> **LEO**
> (*shouts, in tears*)

No. And you're a bastard to use the poor wretches in Bosnia as your excuse!

Paco says nothing. He's continued getting dressed with his back to Leo. Leo goes over to the other side of the bed, crosses the room and sits on the bed, by the bedside table, covered in photos and books, with her back to the rest of the room. The two partners have their backs to each other.

85

You volunteered for the Peace Mission to escape the war you've got here! And I'm the only victim in that war!

Stealthily, Paco picks up the trousers to his uniform, and returns to the bathroom. Leo doesn't realize she's alone in the bedroom and continues reeling off her string of reproaches.

From the moment you decided to join the NATO International Forces you started separating from me . . . people go to Bosnia as volunteers. You could have stayed in your office at the Defence Ministry, if you'd wanted . . . at least until we'd worked out how to solve our problems! But you just wanted to escape from me. Why not have the courage to recognize that, hey?

Stockstill, Leo waits for a reply that never comes.

(*insistently*)

Answer me!

She gets up and turns to the corner of the room where Paco was getting dressed. Discovering she's alone with her reproaches, she flies into a rage. Her fury focuses on the bedside table. She sees the photo of the kiss, picks it up, smashes it against the floor. There are lots of blue marbles lodged in the metal squares of the frame. As it smashes, the marbles bounce on the tiles and roll across the bedroom floor.

INT. LEO'S PLACE, AFTERNOON

Leo is sitting at her desk in her study. Her head in her hands, paralysed by grief. The tension acts like an anaesthetic. She starts typing.

'*If only I could always hate him like I hate him now. The hatred would help me to drive him out of my life. I have to cling to this hatred like a red-hot nail . . . Please, God, help me, though I'm not a believer.*'

Paco appears dressed, holding some clothes in his hand (or in a bag).

Leo seems calmer, anaesthetized.

Paco says nothing.

In a reasonable, matter-of-fact tone, Leo asks him:

LEO

Leaving already?

PACO

Yes.

LEO

Won't you have something to eat?

Leo sounds sad, but at first sight she seems quite normal, except for her sudden weariness.

PACO

No.

They look at each other, like two mindless idiots, with infinitely lugubrious expressions. Hermetic, distanced by their respective feelings of grief. After a pause, Leo looks at the clock.

LEO

Of the two hours which are my due, you still owe me thirty minutes.

Paco reckons her comment is in the worst possible taste, but says nothing. In this way he allows her to dig her own grave . . .

(*with a half-hearted, pathetic smile*)
We've surpassed ourselves this time, haven't we?

PACO

Particularly you.

LEO
(*gentle and sincere*)
Paco, please give me at least twenty-four hours, really. Wherever. However. As soon as possible. You tell me.

PACO

I don't think I can stand another twenty-four hours like this last lot.

LEO

Couldn't we talk it over calmly, like two adults?

PACO

No.

Leo starts another attack of sobbing.

I'd be grateful if you didn't cry in front of me.

Quite unintentionally, Paco is terribly cruel. Leo tries to hold back her tears. The result is grim. Her voice is reduced to a thin whine, strangled by her words.

LEO
(*her face distorted by her sobbing*)

I'd like you to know I am trying.

PACO

I'm off.

Leo gets up and follows him.

LEO
(*stammering*)

Tell me . . . first . . . how do we stand . . .

PACO

I don't know.

He heads for the door, followed by Leo.

LEO

I need to know if you're interested in saving this thing of ours.

INT. LEO'S HOUSE. BY THE DOOR. STILL INSIDE THE HOUSE

Paco picks up his suitcases . . .

PACO

Right now I don't know.

Leo, serious, examines him, and this time can't prevent big tears from rolling down her cheeks.

LEO

In spite of everything . . . I . . . do really want . . .

Leo's words sound like a prayer. Sincere. Paco stays silent. Stands opposite her.

88

Should I read your silence as a total lack of interest?

PACO

Leo . . . don't pressurize me anymore. Can't you see I'm blocked, that I can't speak?

Leo takes a deep breath. Gathers strength. Her lips pucker in hatred and contempt.

LEO

The great strategist . . . you're supposed to be the expert in big conflicts.

Paco is repelled by her comment.

PACO
(*definitively*)

Right, but no war can compare with you.

It's now Leo who stands speechless in front of the door. Paco swings round and walks off. He closes the door. But she opens it.

INT. THE LANDING IN LEO'S HOUSE.

Leo walks on to the landing. The fact that the situation develops outside the flat makes it even more stark and humiliating.

Paco starts going down the stairs. Leo's voice halts him in his tracks, a passionate, swooning howl.

LEO

I'm slow, often I don't understand what's going on, but give me an answer for fuck's sake! Is there the faintest possibility . . . we can save this thing of ours?

Paco stands and looks for her. For some strange reason, at that moment he finds the strength to respond.

PACO

No. None at all.

Leo's transfixed on the landing. Without a backward glance Paco walks on down. Disappears round the first bend.

INT. THE LANDING.

Leo, robot-like, in the same place, listening to Paco's footsteps, one by one on the stairs, definitively separating him from her. When she hears the door bang to she spins round, her face awash with tears, and goes back into her flat.

INT. LEO'S FLAT. THE BATHROOM. AFTERNOON

The towels and underwear still strewn over the bathroom floor where moments before Paco had taken a shower, prompt memories which physically pain Leo. Leo doesn't think she can stand it, doesn't even contemplate the possibility. Her only way out is murder, to kill herself and put an end to so much pain. She looks at the Red Cross shaped cupboard, opens it and picks out from the various bottles of medicine a phial of sleeping-pills or sedatives, whichever might be the most effective. She opens it and empties it on the shelf above the wash-basin. The telephone rings. It's Betty's simpering, ingratiating voice. Leo listens to her message as it records on the answer-machine.

> BETTY
> (*voice-over*)

Leo, darling! Are you around . . . ? Or are you busy?

> *Leo listens to the voice as if she were looking at it from somewhere remote, from another world.*

> (*voice-over*)

It's nothing urgent, but I've got to talk to you. Just for a moment, OK? Are you sure you're not there? Come on, give me a ring.

And she hangs up.

Leo starts taking the pills, slowly, like a robot. In no hurry.

She lies on the bed in her bedroom.

The telephone rings again. As she rapidly slides into unconsciousness, Leo can still hear the caller's voice. Might it be Paco? No. It's her mother.

> MOTHER
> (*voice-over*)

Leo! my darling Leo! Aren't you in? I've had a row with your sister

and I'm off home to the village tomorrow. I'm ringing to say
goodbye . . .

>   (*her tone of voice shows she's whimpering as she speaks*)
My blood pressure's way up, I'll have an attack any moment . . . !
Ring me   . . . ! And don't take any notice of what Rosa says. It's
so sad, my love! She's as nutty as your aunt Petra. Aren't you in? I
really wanted to get this off my chest to you . . . All right, now you
know. Your mother.

> *Leo opens her eyes and tries to get out of bed. Her mother's voice
> manages to make her aware of what she's just done. If she went
> through with her suicide, it would finish her mother off as well.
> Feebly, she mumbles: 'Mum!'*

> *The thought of her mother forces her to drag herself out of bed and
> towards the bathroom. She stumbles along. Sticks the fingers of her
> right hand to the bottom of her throat, provoking terrific retching. She
> throws up, manages to bring up most of the pills she has swallowed,
> mixed up with bits of food. Totters from wall to wall, finally makes it
> to the bath. She pulls the curtain back, her arm weighs so heavily
> that in the end she pulls it down. Seated on the side of the bath she
> turns the cold water tap on, puts her head under and then her whole,
> fully-clothed body. The cold shower starts to revive her. The telephone
> rings again. Betty's back.*

>   **BETTY**
>   (*voice-over*)
Leo? why aren't you answering?
>   (*nervously*)
I'm very worried about you . . . Leo! Please, pick the phone up. If
you don't think something's wrong . . . Leo! I hope that you
haven't done anything crazy! Leo!

INT. A BAR. DUSK

*On the television in the bar we can see the shouting competition that's
held annually in Colmenar de Oreja. A young female competitor
unleashes an extended scream, B-horror movie vintage.*

*With wet hair and a wan face, Leo sits at the bar and watches the
barman adding a good shot of cognac (or whisky), to the coffee he's*

already poured her. Leo drinks it to warm up and wake up. She's wearing ordinary blue jeans, a jersey and a blue overcoat. A red cap and dark glasses complete her outfit.

She looks blankly at the television screen. That must be the competition Angel wanted to invite her to. Might he be watching it live? Thoughts of Angel make her feel linked to life and the world. She also recalls how Angel drank cognac in his coffee when they first met.

Angel.

Now the contestant is older, a typical rural loudmouth. She lets out not a cry of terror, but a very prolonged call.

Two youths dressed in white come in through the door, talking over the incidents on a medical student demonstration.

One of the bar staff shouts that someone should turn that rubbish off. The bartender changes channel. Leo asks for her second coffee with cognac. With her back to the television, she again watches how the bartender pours it out. Suddenly, the sound of a guitar sends a hush through the bar until there's only the sound of Chavela Vargas singing her song, 'En el último trago', (The last gulp) on the television. Her back to the television, Leo feels her blood mixing with the caffeine and alcohol being pumped round by her exhausted heart; she tries to wipe away the first tears with the back of her hand, tears heralding an immediate downpour. 'Help me finish this bottle, we'll leave after the last gulp . . . I want a taste of your indifference . . .'

Leo turns to the television. Chavela's voice, broken and fretted by years of hell, communicates the suffering accumulated by Leo.

'Tonight I'll not beg you. Tonight you're really leaving. It's so hard to see you go, still feeling that you love me.'

Leo weeps unashamedly into her coffee and cognac.

Chavela has opened up within Leo, quite spontaneously, the sluice-gates to a real reservoir of bitterness.

'The years have taught me so much! I go on making the same mistakes. I'll be back drinking with strangers, crying over the same heart- breaks . . .'

EXT. STREET. DUSK

Leo leaves the bar, still haunted by the song. The pavement has been taken over by a crowd of noisy youngsters, dressed in white, flooding the street with their placards, slogans and leaflets. It's a medical students' demonstration. Piles of tiny leaflets fly through the air like hypnotized butterflies. An expert demonstrator has let them go on a sudden breeze. Between the din and the paper, Leo weeps her heart out. Nobody looks at her and she sees no one.

All dressed in white, the students chant a range of slogans: 'Now Felipe's going to cure the flu! Take Felipe to the dissecting room! All we students want in life is a contract and no fucking about! Don't fuck us here! Don't fuck us there! Don't fuck us everywhere!'

Leo walks by a bathroom showroom. A variety of merchandise is on display. There's an advertising ditty stuck along the bottom of the front window in transparent adhesive: 'I love you. ♥ *Rock.' Leo manages to read the slogan through her tears. It's the last straw. She almost runs off, in flight from her memories. She bumps violently into someone while making her escape. Leo loses her balance as a result of the collision and almost falls over. The body she's crashed into belongs to Angel.*

ANGEL
(frightened)

Leo, what's the matter?

Leo hugs him and rests her head against his chest.

Angel doesn't flinch. He doesn't mind people looking at them. He'll stand there, with his arms round Leo, until her tears run dry. The demonstration moves off towards the spot where the couple's standing, sweeps them up into its bosom. Leo and Angel's encounter seems to have escaped from a film musical, the scene also has touches of carnival extravaganza and nightmarish baroque.

INT. ANGEL'S HOUSE. DAY

The following day, at about twelve, Leo wakes up on the sixteenth floor of the Palace of the Press building, in Plaza Callao. She opens her eyes and looks wearily around. She doesn't recognize anything in what she can see, except her own anguish. She feels ill, and not just because of her

95

hangover. She coughs. Without moving from the bed she tries to find an image to connect her to where she is, but fails. She hears noises.

The space is a diaphanous Madrid loft, its huge round or semicircular windows open over the roof-tops of the Gran Vía. Leo's bedhead is one of these windows that spring from the floor and end in a semicircle. Behind Leo, the window is curtainless, giving the impression of a woman who has woken up on the edge of the abyss.

On the soundtrack Bola de Nieve is singing 'The Pain of Living'.

The clean, elegant floor preserves the charm of the original. The walls, on the other hand, are self-consciously bare, the result of being stripped of their original covering. Shelves of books and bric-à-brac. Few pieces of furniture and lots of books and magazines, video tapes, etc. piled high. The individual world of a contemporary bohemian. The place seems both simple and excessive, warm, decrepit and spectacular. Madrid floods in through every window.

The sounds Leo can hear come from the kitchen. Angel, in better shape than she is, places a red rose inside a small glass of water. The glass is part of a tray laden with healthy food and drinks (Buns, coffee, alka seltzer, water, fruit juices, unopened beer, etc.).

Angel carries the tray from the kitchen, in a corner separated from the rest of the space by an attractive bar, over to the bed which hovers over the abyss. Plaza Callao roars down below.

Upon seeing him, Leo attempts a faint, weary, questioning smile.

LEO

Angel?

ANGEL

Good morning. Well, how are you?

Leo lets out something like a bellow that finally subsides into a hoarse grunt.

LEO

Very poorly . . .

Angel puts the tray down next to the patient.

What are we doing here?

Leo looks at the tray and makes it clear it's unappetizing.

ANGEL

We're in my new place, and are about to have breakfast.

Leo looks at the space once more. She's evidently not complaining for the sake of it. She looks very ill.

LEO

I can't remember anything . . .

ANGEL

I do. I remember everything and I'm going to blackmail you . . .

He opens a can of beer and drinks.

LEO

Blackmail?

ANGEL

Look through the window.

Leo obeys. Opposite the building where Angel lives, at the other end of Plaza Callao, the FNAC (French Bookshop) is covered by an enormous publicity poster for Amanda Gris's 'Anthology'. After looking at the FNAC façade Leo turns to Angel.

LEO

I expect I drank and said too much yesterday.

ANGEL

You did. Among other things you revealed to me 'the flower of your secret' . . . as Amanda Gris would say. Forget I'm a journalist. I won't do anything, on one condition . . .

LEO
(*very fragile*)

What?

ANGEL
(*serious*)

Promise you won't try to repeat what you did yesterday . . . and that you'll share your secret with me.

Leo's tears start to well up.

97

All right?

LEO
(*stops sniffling*)

All right.

INT. LEO'S HOME

Angel's with Leo. On the surface, she seems relaxed. In reality, she's exhausted and very limp, pale and expressionless, like an automaton. It's very difficult to take the strain of so much reality. Leo knows that the door now being opened was, the previous day, shut and hermetically sealed on her and Paco.

Angel is a chance, but sympathetic (almost enthusiastic), witness of everything that's going to happen next. A privileged spectator and pleased to be so. Leo opens up, frightened by the power of her memories. Not sure she can stand them. Fragile, very fragile.

A scream greets them as soon as the door is opened.

BETTY

Leo!

More distraught and more lacerated by exhaustion than Leo, Betty comes out to welcome them. She's less formally dressed then we have seen her before. Wrinkled and out-of-sorts, as if she's just come down from a bad trip.

LEO

You frightened me, Betty!

BETTY
(*roars angrily*)

I frightened you? That's rich!

LEO
(*not even taken aback*)
And you still frighten me. What are you doing here?

BETTY

I've been out the whole night looking for you. Where've you been?
(*shrieking*)

Why didn't you ring me?

That comes out as rather more than a reproach. A prisoner of her own problems, Leo doesn't understand what she's referring to. The previous night she wasn't in a state to be thinking about Betty.

LEO

Why?

BETTY
(*not letting up*)

I rang round the hospitals, the police . . . I had half the city on your tracks!

LEO

Don't shout, my head's killing me!

The atmosphere in the house has drained Leo of the little strength she had left. Angel heads for the kitchen.

ANGEL
(*to Leo*)

Do you want a beer? It'll go down well.

LEO

Thanks. I've given up drinking.

ANGEL
(*to Betty*)

Well, you should take a sedative.

LEO
(*gravely*)

None left. I took them all last night.

BETTY
(*still very agitated*)

So, as I thought, you tried to commit suicide!

LEO

Let's forget all that, Betty.

BETTY

That's the trouble, you never want to mention 'all that', or let anyone else have their say.

LEO

Have you got something new to tell me?

BETTY

Aren't you wondering how I got in? Who gave me the keys?
(*Leo looks at her questioningly, waits for a reply*)
Paco! Or didn't you think it odd he phoned me the other day
when you were at my place?

LEO

Wasn't it me he phoned?

BETTY

No!

Leo goes quiet, looks into space.

What do we have to do to make you face up to reality?

*Betty carries on out of pure momentum. She doesn't really need an
answer.*

Hey? What do we have to do to make you accept reality?

LEO
(*faint, with no undue emphasis*)
To . . . for the rest of you . . . not to hide it from me.

BETTY

How can we say anything if your world falls apart because your
boots are too tight! Paco's been trying to talk to you for years . . .
but before he ever got started, you were screaming like a woman
demented. And Paco's not that cruel.

LEO

Why didn't you tell me? You're the expert.

BETTY

At what?

LEO

At bad news . . . you even give seminars to doctors.

Leo's words have everything except humour.

BETTY

I'm telling you now.

LEO

Fine. Well now you've told me, be so good as to leave.

BETTY
(*devastated*)

No . . . I won't go . . .

Leo looks at her, too weak to throw her out.

In case you're interested. I've also broken with him . . . and I did so on your behalf. When he came last night and told me about the row . . . I asked him how he'd dared to leave you alone, in such a state. He insisted it was your natural state, but I know you better and I imagined what you felt like. So I threw him out, got the keys from him, and came here so you wouldn't be alone. When I saw the vomit and the empty bottle of sedatives I imagined the worst. You don't know what I've suffered . . .

She cries, lets go; no longer hysterical, her nerves finally release the tension pent up over the last few hours.

LEO
(*dry-eyed*)

Does he know?

BETTY
(*still crying*)

Yes, he phoned this morning from the airport, before he got on the plane.

LEO

It's definite he's off to Split?

BETTY

Yes, he must be there by now.

LEO
(*a simple, direct monotone*)

How long have you been lovers?

BETTY
(*quite naturally*)

It was . . . just before he decided to go to Brussels. Paco came to
see me. You were in total crisis as well and he couldn't bear the
idea of seeing you suffer. He no longer loved you, but didn't know
how to tell you. He came to me as a friend of yours and as a
psychologist. I told him that precisely because I was your friend I
couldn't accept him as a patient. I recommended him to a
colleague . . . but I don't know whether they ever saw each other.
Paco went on visiting me . . . he liked getting it out of his system,
on a friend-to-friend basis. Until somehow or other, one day we
ended up in each other's arms . . .

*Leo listens stony-faced, making no comment, almost unflinching. The
telephone rings. Leo stays still.*

The telephone . . .

LEO

So I hear.

BETTY

Won't you take it?

LEO

No, you take it, it's for you. Tell him I've turned up and that I've
been informed. But wait till I'm out of here, please . . .

*Leo gets up, turning towards Angel, who's stayed quiet, clutching his
beer by the door leading from Leo's study to the lounge. Betty pounces
joyfully on the receiver, looking towards the door through which Leo
has just disappeared.*

BETTY
(*cheerfully*)

Yes . . . ?
(*disappointed*)
Oh, she'll come rightaway . . .
(*shouting*)
Leo! Your mother!

*Leo comes round, she'd forgotten about her, returns to where Betty is
and takes the phone. She tries to sound firm in her tone and attitude.*

103

Angel observes them, ever thirsty.

                    LEO
Mum! I was just thinking of ringing you . . .

INT. ROSA'S HOUSE. DAY

Their mother whimpering into the phone . . .

                    MOTHER
Oh my love. It's so sad! If only your father could rise from the
dead.

                    LEO
Mum, don't cry. I'm coming to take you to the village right now.
And I'll come too!

                    MOTHER
          (*shouts excitedly, on the verge of a heart-attack*)
My love! My dear, dear daughter!

                    LEO
I'll stay as long as you need me.

                    MOTHER
               (*crying*)
I don't want to make it hard for you, I know you've got plenty on
your . . .

   Rosa takes the telephone from her, also verging on the hysteric.

                    ROSA
Leo, don't take any notice! Nobody's thrown her out of here!

                    LEO
          (*making a superhuman effort*)
I know, Rosa.

                    ROSA
Her mind's a complete blank . . . ! I can't do any more than what
I'm already doing!

   *Rosa and her mother get involved in a new squabble, the perennial
   one, but now more heated than usual. Leo thinks quickly. She can't
   think how to shut them up. She just says:*

LEO
You'll soon be able to tell me everything. I'm on my way.

On the point of collapse . . .

EXT. A MAIN ROAD. DAY

Angel's driving. Leo and her mother are in the back seat. Leo looks terrible, really ill. Quite heart-broken, though she's trying to hide the fact.

Her mother tells Angel that this craze for slimming . . . she blames Leo's poorly state on lack of food.

LEO
(*totally drained*)
Mum, please . . .

MOTHER
Look at her, she can hardly speak. Don't you start dieting, Angel, you're very handsome as you are.

Angel smiles at Leo's mother's comments. She cheers him up.

ANGEL
Don't worry . . . I'm a big eater . . .

MOTHER

She was a plump little thing. When she was born, she weighed five and quarter kilos, after two days' labour. Choking to death when she popped out . . . ! And thanks to my sergeant-major of a mother-in-law – may she rest in peace – who said: 'Take the girl into the yard!' I said: 'But it's freezing! You don't know how cold it gets out in these yards in winter!' But because she was such a sergeant-major, we carried my little girl into the yard, she responded and was saved . . .

Silent, motionless, her gaze hidden behind dark glasses, Leo listens to her mother, making an effort not to break down in front of her. She's thinking how she's had to struggle to survive from day one.

MOTHER
(*to Leo*)

Do you remember, Leocadia?

LEO
(*a wisp of a voice*)

Mum, how could I ever remember that?

MOTHER

No, I meant the poem I wrote for the village.

Such a beautiful morning, Leo,
a sparkling sun,
flowers perfuming the air
the rustle of orchard leaves

Leo isn't prepared for this. It lays her low. She looks through the window so her mother won't see her crying, as she continues her recitation:

Chirping from branch to branch
the cheerful little birdies
flutter and fly
enchant me with their song.
We hear the bleat-bleat
of the flocks of sheep,
scattered over the grass
like snow-flakes
Here there's a hut
that's a shepherd's home
there's a little white house
whiter than an Easter lily.
Further on a farmhouse
next to the farmhouse an orchard
next to the orchard a house
next to the house the church.
The hills are full of oak-trees,
the valleys ripe with fruit
the river's lined by trees
You've guessed? It's my village.

Angel drives into the village.

EXT. THE MOTHER'S STREET. DUSK. THE VILLAGE

The car turns into the street where Leo's mother lives. They've hardly come to a halt before two or three women neighbours who heard them drive up open their front-doors. They wait shamelessly to see who gets out of the car. First it's Angel, who opens the door for the mother and helps her get out. The neighbours walk over delighted.

Jacinta!

When we heard the car we said, reckon it stopped where old
Jacinta . . .

*Beside herself with happiness, the mother kisses her neighbours. Leo
opens her door and gets out of the car, ghostly pale.*

MOTHER
(<i>pleased</i>)</div>

My Leo has come with me!

*Leo looks at the neighbours trying to smile and participate in some
way in the general good spirits. Before she's able to say hello she
collapses to the ground. Angel immediately stoops down and picks her
up. The neighbours crowd round and try to help her, exclaiming
loudly.*

ANGEL

No need, I can do it myself . . .

He takes her in his arms and says to her mother,

Ma'am, open the door
(to her mother)

*The mother opens the door whilst the neighbours comment. 'She looked
really awful', 'I get car-sick as well'. Angel carries Leo in his arms.*

They go inside, under the neighbours' watchful eyes.

*They look like a pair of newly-weds going in the bedroom on their
wedding-night.*

At least that's how Angel feels.

INT. NIGHT. THE MOTHER'S HOUSE. IN LA MANCHA

*Leo still feels sick. She's in bed (documentation on alcohol withdrawal
symptoms and the recovery time for a person with medium addiction.)
By her bedside table, there's a steaming cup of broth.*

Her mother comes over, looks at the cup and sits on the edge of the bed.

MOTHER

But you've not touched the broth . . . what's wrong, Leo?

LEO

I'm going mad, Mum.

MOTHER

(*trying to console her*)

Your sister is, you're not.

LEO

Right, like our aunts, like grandmother. Mad.

MOTHER

It's Paco, isn't it . . .?

Leo doesn't reply. Her silence and the way she looks into the void are enough. Her mother lifts her right hand to her forehead very expressively.

Just what I was thinking, just what I was thinking . . . Such a pity, my love! So young, yet already like a cow without its cow-bell!

LEO

What do you mean a cow without its cow-bell . . . ?

MOTHER

I mean . . . lost . . . wandering, aimless, like me . . .

LEO

Like you?

MOTHER

I too am like a cow without its cow-bell, but it's more normal at my age . . . That's why I want to live here, in the village. When a husband leaves his wife because he's died or gone off with another woman, for it makes no odds . . . we must go back to where we were born . . . visit the local hermitage, chat on the doorstep with the neighbours, go to evening prayers with them, even though you're not a believer . . . because if we don't, we lose our way like a cow without its bell.

Many things come together at that moment for Leo. Her loneliness. And her mother's.

LEO

Mum . . .

MOTHER

Oh my love, it was such an effort getting you on the road . . . !

INT. THE MOTHER'S HOUSE. IN LA MANCHA. WEEKS LATER

Leo looks much better. The suffering has left her much more subdued. Her mother is showing her an envelope that she's brought down from the attic, it contains hundreds of sheets of paper. They're the typing exercises Leo used to do as a child. The pages are divided into blocks, made up of frequently repeated words or sentences. They remind Leo of the memory drills she's recently been writing in Madrid. She can't see much difference between one end of the cycle and another. The literature or the handwriting.

*[Leo sits watching a group of old women – friends of her mother –

LEO

Tell me. What do you call the ones with the large heads?

FELIPA

Pins.

LEO

And the others?

FELIPA

Needles.

LEO

Of course.

FELIPA

Don't you know the proverb?

LEO

Which one?

FELIPA

The one that goes: 'Jealousy pricks like a needle. Jealousy drives me crazy. If you want to know about jealousy, just ask me.'

*Scene added during filming.

110

LEO

Or me . . . What ever became of Aunt Valentina?

FELIPA

She threw herself down the well.

LEO

She what? Down the well?

FELIPA

That's right. Threw herself down the well.

LEO

You mean: killed herself.

FELIPA

Right. She stayed there a long time till some building workers
found her and asked her son to go and take a look. They got her
out and . . .

PILAR

Hey, I didn't know you had an aunt.

LEO

Oh, she was marvellous. She used to tell me such fantastic stories.

OLD WOMAN

She was really nice, hardworking but lonely . . .

FELIPA

She was very pretty, tall, and was very, you know . . .

LEO

Come on. Sing me a song. Before I get really depressed . . .

WOMEN

Which song?

LEO

What's it called? The song . . . about belonging to Almagro.

WOMEN

All right. Come on then!

I'm from Almagro, I'm from Almagro.
I'm from fertile land
where we make lace
and cook egg-plants
cook egg-plants
cook egg-plants
I'm from Almagro, I'm from Almagro
I'm from fertile land . . .

MOTHER
(*arriving breathless*)

Leocadia, someone on the phone for you.]

INT. HER MOTHER'S HOUSE. A VILLAGE IN LA MANCHA. DAY

*Leo goes into the house. Picks up the receiver. It's Alicia. Leo doesn't
show how surprised she is.*

LEO

How did you get hold of my telephone number?

ALICIA

You gave it me, with your last story . . . Don't you remember?

LEO
(*pretending*)

Oh, of course, my last offering.

Leo hesitates, doesn't know which offering she's referring to. Alicia notices nothing odd, is charming and entirely unsuspicious.

ALICIA

We really liked your last two novels, Leo! The best you've written in a long while. Unadulterated Amanda Gris!

LEO
(*at a loss*)

I'm so pleased. . .!

ALICIA

Hey, I read they're shooting a film with a story-line identical to the Cold Store one. I forgot to mention it to you.

LEO

I read that as well.

ALICIA

A pretty big coincidence, don't you think?

LEO

I don't know . . .

ALICIA

Tomás suggested . . . I don't believe him, but . . . You know how crude he is . . . You didn't sell it under another name, did you?

LEO

Me? When you rejected it, I put it in a drawer, and it's still there.

ALICIA

Of course . . . Could anyone have stolen it?

LEO

In no way. But . . . come to think of it . . . Alicia . . . you're the only person who's got another copy. Perhaps it was stolen from you?

ALICIA

From me? And who might that have been?

LEO

Your son . . . the junkie . . . it wouldn't be his first theft . . .
> (*not allowing her to interrupt her*)

He'd photocopy it in an hour. Remember how bad you thought it was, I didn't even copyright it . . .

ALICIA

Why not?

LEO

Well . . . Why would I copyright such rubbish?

ALICIA

Leo, you copyright rubbish along with everything else!
> (*embarrassed*)

I'll ask my son . . . but best forget all this.

LEO

Yes.

ALICIA

The important news is that Amanda Gris is back on form!

LEO

Yes. That's the important news!

INT. ANGEL'S HOUSE. INT. THE MOTHER'S HOUSE. DAY

Angel is typing. The telephone rings. He picks it up.

LEO
> (*voice-over*)

Angel, it's Leo.

ANGEL

Leo! Great!

Alternate images of both of them in their respective houses. Leo is calling from her mother's.

LEO

Did you give the Fascination people my telephone number? Alicia just phoned me.

ANGEL

Yes

(*guiltily*)

. . . I gave it to her . . . So what?

LEO

She told me she'd received two novels by Amanda Gris, and I can assure you I didn't write them and I haven't had a drink for months, so I'm not delirious!

ANGEL

You didn't tell her that?

LEO

No . . . Why?

ANGEL

(*sighs*)

Wow! Just as well.

LEO

Did you write them?

ANGEL

Yes . . .

(*anxiously*)

Don't tell me they didn't like them! They noticed the difference and rejected them! That's awful!

LEO

(*shouts out, shocked*)

No! They're thrilled to bits, Angel! They think they're better than ever! But . . . how did you dare to send them, without telling me first?

ANGEL

I was afraid you'd reject the idea. I'm sorry, but cheer up. You're free! When are you coming back to Madrid?

LEO

Soon, I'm afraid. Paco has already started separation proceedings.

ANGEL

Give me a ring. I really want to see you.

From her expression, the idea of going back doesn't appeal.

LEO

Fine, I'll ring you. But I don't like you doing these things without telling me, OK?

EXT. MADRID. THEATRE. NIGHT

Weeks later.

The façade of an independent theatre, Olympia Hall style. In the area ticket-holders hustle and bustle, generally young people, with a variety of tribal allegiances. Angel stands there looking nervously from one side of the street to another, waiting anxiously. Next to him, on the façade, a poster advertising Blanca and Antonio's show. They head the cast and Antonio is credited as choreographer. At last Angel spots Leo in the distance.

They meet up and kiss, etc. He looks her up and down. Leo seems better than the last time he saw her, though he looks worse. He's been drinking, and it shows.

ANGEL

How did it go with the lawyer?

LEO

Very unpleasant.

ANGEL

You look fantastic.

LEO
(*sweetly*)

You don't.

ANGEL

It must be emotional.

INT. THEATRE

In their respective seats. Surrounded by people being ushered to theirs. Leo is holding a programme. They're talking about Amanda.

LEO

Angel, I'm very grateful. But I don't want to take advantage of you.

116

ANGEL

It's not the first time I've been a ghost writer.

LEO

Well, it's the first time someone has done my writing for me.

ANGEL

You'll soon get used to it . . . It's very relaxing!

LEO

Sure, but what about you?

ANGEL

I've always dreamed about being Barbara Cartland.

LEO

You're so happy-go-lucky! How long will that keep you amused?

ANGEL

As a minimum, till your contract runs out.

LEO

You want something in exchange, I expect . . .

ANGEL

It wasn't bothering me, but if you insist.

LEO

I do insist.

Angel thinks it over, but says nothing. He doesn't dare ask for what he'd really like in exchange.

ANGEL

I don't dare.

LEO

Come on. Name your price.

ANGEL

A price . . .? You can keep twenty per cent of the proceeds like an agent. And I'll keep eighty per cent. What do you think?

LEO

Agreed!

THE SHOW

Antonio and Blanca are alone on stage dancing a 'Soleá' by Miles Davis. It's originally and brilliantly choreographed. It makes a huge impact on Leo. She'd never imagined they had so much talent.

It's a minimal set. Subtle. Simple. Cheap and beautiful. The lighting's perfect. Blanca is a profound, original dancer. Her movements suggest something both ancestral and very stylised. Physically she seems transformed. Leo can't believe she's the same woman who months ago had cooked her meals and washed her clothes. Antonio also looks quite different, exudes sexual attractiveness. Both the choreography and the routine he dances with his mother are wonderfully carried through. Neither gives the impression of being a novice. In fact, they're not. A deep feeling for flamenco, fused with swing; a perfect match, two sides of the same coin. Angel looks at Leo. Registers her emotion. Takes out a flask and has a swig. She's so absorbed in what's happening on stage that she doesn't even notice.

INT. THE THEATRE DRESSING-ROOMS. NIGHT

Blanca, still in her stage make-up, is greeting some friends, including Rosa, Leo's sister, who is dressed in her Sunday best. She's with a hairdresser neighbour. The group notices Leo coming towards the changing room, accompanied by a rather tipsy Angel, who tactfully keeps to the sidelines during the rest of the sequence. The two sisters greet each other, enraptured, they were not expecting to meet.

LEO

Rosa!

ROSA

Leo! What a surprise!

LEO

I got here from the village today.

ROSA

I know, Mum told me. How'd it go with the lawyer?

LEO

Huh . . . All right . . .

(*to Blanca*)

Blanca!

Leo kisses and hugs Blanca.

What a marvellous show! You can't imagine how it moved me.

ROSA

Really? Who'd have thought it!

Leo introduces them.

LEO
(*to Blanca*)

This is my sister Rosa.

ROSA

We know each other already . . .

LEO

Oh, do you?

ROSA

Of course . . . We spoke so often on the phone that we became friends.

BLANCA

Rosa kept me up to date with what was going on in the village.

ROSA

And she told me about what was going on here.

BLANCA
(*to Rosa*)

Why didn't you tell me she was coming to Madrid today!

ROSA

I only found out this afternoon.

BLANCA

Her fridge'll be empty and the house'll be filthy.

Antonio comes out of the bathroom, his hair sopping wet.

Antonio! Look who's here!

Antonio looks at Leo, stunned. He looks more mature, more manly.

More attractive. More complete. Leo smiles at him. Antonio regains his confidence. They welcome each other with a kiss, at her initiative.

Angel witnesses all this, but doesn't join the group, he stays on the sidelines.

ANTONIO

Did you like it?

LEO

Of course I liked it! I've got a guilty conscience about wasting so much of your time . . . How could I imagine my maid was such a terrific artist . . . And as for you!

BLANCA

Madam helped us more than she thinks.

ANTONIO

And she's still frightened before she's out on . . .

BLANCA
(*to Rosa*)

I'd not danced for such a long time!
(*to Leo*)

That doesn't mean I won't be round to sort out her house in the morning.

EXT. THE STREET. NIGHT

Angel and Leo walk silently along. Angel kicks various cardboard boxes he finds littering the ground. Leo looks at him, and frowns. When Angel notices he stops playing with the boxes.

ANGEL

Anything the matter?

LEO
(*seriously*)

No . . .

ANGEL

Nothing at all. You were slobbering in the dressing-rooms. And now . . . you are going to start crying. Am I so unpleasant to be with?

121

LEO

Watching you kicking the boxes reminded me of Paco. Three
years ago we went to Athens. It's not like Madrid, there are almost
no bars. We were walking along the street by ourselves. Paco was
playing football, like you just now, with cardboard boxes. He was
like a kid . . . that's the only happy memory I've got from that trip.

ANGEL
(*too emphatically*)

A total ban on football! From now on I'll only dance . . . If
spinning tops can dance, so can I!

Leo smiles.

*Angel starts dancing in the middle of the street, imitating Antonio.
One pirouette and he slumps to the ground. He's more drunk than
Leo had thought.*

*She goes over and tries to lift him up. But it's hard work, Angel is
very heavy. Once he's on his feet, Angel leans his head on Leo's
shoulder, embarrassed or perhaps to hide his sadness. Together they
create an image similar to the one they made during the
demonstration in the street.*

(*his face still hidden against Leo's shoulder*)

Do you remember *Casablanca*? The first time Ingrid Bergman
goes into Rick's diner? They both sit down at the same table.
Humphrey Bogart is rigid, expressionless, he's so moved.

*Leo looks at him attentively, expectantly but wanting him to get it
over with. As is usually the case with drunks, it's difficult to catch his
drift. Angel moves his head away from her shoulder and looks at her.*

Ingrid asks him if he remembers the last time they saw each other.
It was in Paris. Bogart replies woodenly: 'I remember every detail.
(It was the day the Germans occupied Paris.) The Germans wore
grey, you wore blue . . .'

Leo looks at Angel intensely, still wondering what he's driving at.

You wore blue the day you were running away from your life and
collided with mine.

The day Angel's referring to was the last time Leo saw her husband,

122

the day of her attempted suicide; the memory produces a pain that time alone has been able to heal.

LEO
(rather violently)
I refuse to remember that day!

ANGEL
Well, I shall always remember it.

Leo conceals her unease. She tries not to get annoyed with the drunken Angel, but can't stop her tone getting harsher. Their memory of that day separates them. She concludes their night out is over.

LEO
(matter-of-fact)
Come on, Angel, I'll take you home.

ANGEL
Stay with me.

LEO
No. I must go home.

ANGEL
By yourself?

LEO
Yes.

Leo sounds more and more decisive. Angel is hurt, and when this happens he gets ironic.

ANGEL
How strong you've become! I preferred you when you were fragile!

LEO
(reining in her temper)
I still am, my suit-cases are still in the car because I didn't dare carry them upstairs. I'm not strong at all! But I've got to learn to live in that place without Paco!

ANGEL
Let's go and have a drink then. Alcohol will give you courage.

LEO
(decisively)

I've also got to learn to live without alcohol . . . without Paco and without alcohol. And the sooner I get started the better!

>   *Leo turns round and leaves Angel in the worst company possible: alone with himself.*

INT. LEO'S PLACE. NIGHT

Leo opens the door to her flat. Closes it.

She stands motionless for a moment. She doesn't know what she'll find. But it's predictable: she finds only solitude.

She leaves the cases in the hall. Initially she sees things belonging to Paco that are no longer there. Absences. She takes a deep breath. Reviving herself. She's not sure she can take another step. The entryphone rings. She gives a start. Intrigued she walks over to the kitchen, where there's a small entryphone on the wall. She thinks it may be Paco. Or Angel.

The bell rings again. Leo gets very close. She berates it as if it were a person.

LEO

I'm not going to answer.

>   *But immediately contradicts herself and picks it up.*

Who's that?

ANTONIO
(voice-over)

It's Antonio.   ———

LEO

Antonio?

ANTONIO
(voice-over)

Will you open up?

>   *Still not fully with it, Leo presses the automatic entry button.*

124

INT. THE HALLWAY

A little later she opens the door for Antonio. Leo looks out on to the landing, Antonio is closing the lift. Before he gets to the door:

LEO

What's the matter, Antonio?

ANTONIO

My mother made me bring you something.

Antonio is carrying two bags, one of food and another of drink.

LEO

Come in. But why did you bother at this time of night!

Antonio walks in. They both go to the kitchen. While they talk, Antonio helps her put the things in the fridge.

ANTONIO

You know what she's like . . .

Leo looks at the bottle of whisky.

LEO

Whisky! I've given it up, you know? But I'm ready to get back into it, if you'll join me. Do you want a glass? Say you do.

ANTONIO

Of course.

Silently, Leo pours out two glasses, neat.

LEO

I've no ice, all right?

ANTONIO

OK. Are you going to sleep here tonight?

LEO

Yes. At least I'm going to try.

ANTONIO

By yourself?

LEO

Yes, why?

ANTONIO

Do you want me to stay with you?

A surprise. And very timely. One Leo wasn't expecting. She takes refuge in wit to avoid responding and to hide her surprise.

LEO

If you're daring to suggest what I think you are, you ought to have the nerve to use 'tú' when you speak to me.

ANTONIO

All right, do you (*tú*) want me to stay with you (*tú*)?

LEO

Antonio, don't put me to the test.
                    (*looks at him*)
Come on, drink up and clear off. Salud!

Leo knocks her glass against Antonio's, thinking 'what a nerve . . .'

ANTONIO
                    (*drinks*)
First, I've got a confession to make . . .
                    (*very seriously*)

LEO

If you're going to tell me that ever since that first time you saw me, throwing up in this passageway, you've been crazy for my carcass . . . spare yourself the confession!

ANTONIO

No, it's not that.
                    (*gravely*)
I've stolen some things from you
                    (*reverting to the formal* usted)

LEO

Such as?

ANTONIO

Small, unimportant things.

LEO

While I was out?

No. You were in. Taking advantage of the fact you were in a state
of amnesia. I collected what I could. I also took the novel about
the 'Cold Store' out of the rubbish bin. I gave it to a friend, who
got it typed out again and sold it to a producer. They're filming it,
I don't know if you'd cottoned on . . .

LEO

Yes. I read that . . .

(*thoughtfully*)

So it was you?

ANTONIO

(*point of information*)

But I'm not a thief.

LEO

(*ironically*)

No, of course not . . .

ANTONIO

(*explaining*)

We used the money to set the show up. It was the only way to
finance it and I was fed up with working the flamenco clubs.

LEO

Hey, was your mother stealing as well?

ANTONIO

(*scandalized*)

My mother. Never! She's totally anti-theft! She knew nothing.
When she found out, she got really . . .! Do you remember the day
Don Paco came?

LEO

Yes, dear, I do.

ANTONIO

It was the day you found us squabbling . . .

LEO

Yes, the day of the paella.

ANTONIO

That was because the day before she'd caught me stealing in here
. . . And she didn't want to perform . . . My mother is nuts about
you.

LEO
(*all emotional*)

I am about her too.

Leo keeps on drinking. Ruminating. Reflecting.

ANTONIO

She keeps reminding me of the big debt we owe you.

LEO
(*it suddenly occurs to her*)

And so you came here tonight to pay it off . . .

Antonio says nothing. Drinks.

How many fucks do you think would have paid it off? What am I
worth?

ANTONIO
(*shamefaced, begging her*)

Please don't ask such things. I'll give back all the money to you
. . . when I've got it.

LEO
(*on a more cheerful note*)

It's not necessary. You couldn't have made a better investment
than the wonderful show I saw tonight!

ANTONIO

You really mean that?

LEO
(*punctuating her sentences with various shots of whisky*)

That's life! Cruel, paradoxical, unpredictable and yet, so just!

ANTONIO
(*doesn't understand her*)

If you say so.

Leo's eyes become really animated. It spreads to Antonio.

Well, do I leave or do I stay?

LEO
(*in a good mood*)
No. Finish drinking this glass.
(*pours it out*)
Then off with you. While I'm still in control of myself. Salud!

She clinks her glass against Antonio's. They drink.

She goes to the door with him.

IN THE DOORWAY

LEO
And thanks a lot, Antonio.

ANTONIO
What for?

LEO
For giving meaning to the darkest months of my life. And as a little bonus, you got me to forget Paco . . . I haven't thought about him for a quarter of an hour.

Before Antonio can ask again if he's staying, Leo shuts the door.

INT. ANGEL'S HOUSE

Angel sitting in front of the fireplace. The armchair hides almost the whole of his face. The fire is burning brightly. There's a bottle and glass on a side-table. Angel is drinking and making notes. He hears the doorbell. Goes out to open the door. It's Leo. If he's surprised, he doesn't show it.

He takes Leo into the lounge. Angel sits down in his armchair, she sits in another one, also facing the fireplace, symmetrical with Angel. A pause.

LEO
This reminds me of *Rich and Famous*, the two women-writer friends, drinking a toast, by themselves, far from the madding crowd, in front of an open fire.

ANGEL
But you're off alcohol, and it was New Year's Eve, that's why they were drinking a toast.

Offer me a drink and I'll turn this into New Year's Eve.

Angel pours out a glass. Leo picks it up and takes a sip.

Angel is motionless, calm and very sensitive, almost begging, but there's no pleading in his voice, it's only a murmur.

ANGEL

Kiss me. If it's New Year's Eve I want to feel contact with human flesh . . . and you're the only flesh around here.

The flutes of the Ballad of the Full Moon *begin to play, followed by the dulcet tones of Caetano Veloso.*

Leo goes over to Angel and kisses him on the lips. They separate and offer a toast. The image freezes . . . but the fire's still burning in the hearth. The flame grows. It's the only thing which moves, the rest of the image stays still.

Caetano's voice goes on singing his exquisite ballad to Leo, to Angel and the audience. And he does so tenderly, delicately as if singing a cradle-song.

Epilogue

The Author Reflects

GENESIS

The Flower of My Secret is a film about 'real' feelings, but makes no concession whatsoever to sentimentality. In other words, it's a drama with hard edges. Though I adore melodrama, this time I've gone for the stark and the succinct. A taste of bile, not honey. Tears of desolation, not consolation. Old-fashioned pain and suffering.

This *Flower* . . . gives off an intense, painful scent; yet there are no wicked characters. They're all good people, as in Capra's films. But despite this lack of wickedness, through their awkwardness, indecision or cowardice (or simply because human beings are imperfect), in the end they inflict pain. Almost all of them live as impostors, pretending to be what, in reality, they're not. Of them all, Leo expresses herself the most sincerely. To lie or dissemble, a degree of determination is required, and she's too weak.

Another expression I'm terrified of using (apart from 'real feeling') is the one about 'the story being full of humanity', or 'its characters are brimming with humanity'. But that's how it is, though these expressions have lost their meaning through abuse or misuse.

Of the scripts I've filmed I remember perfectly the first pages I wrote, the ones that were to be the seed and driving-force of future films. My initial impulse is to make a short from those first pages, but in the end I always turn them into a feature film, not just because it's more profitable but also because these first pages make me tremendously curious about the characters and the situation they are experiencing. If I want to know how they'd got that far and what happens to them afterwards, I am the one who has to find out and write it down. And through investigating the past and future of these characters, I always discover the story that I had wanted to tell but had had no idea of at the beginning. Because of this random system of creation, the first sequences I write nearly always correspond to half of the film they generate.

The first thing I wrote about *Kika* was the whole rape episode, from Paul Bazzo's arrival to his disappearing act through the window. In *High Heels* it was the sequence with Victoria Abril's confession on the news, when she admits she committed the murder. In *Tie Me Up! Tie Me Down!* it was Antonio Banderas's statement after he has isolated and immobilized Victoria Abril: 'I'm twenty-three years old and have got fifty thousand pesetas. I'm alone in the world, I'd like to be a good husband to you and a good father to your children.'

The first sequence I wrote of *The Flower of My Secret*, what I was desperate to see on screen, was the husband's visit. In the (almost) eight versions of the screenplay that I have written, his visit is a sequence which has hardly changed. It just poured out of me, from the moment the husband rings the bell to when he disappears over the landing. You could say I filmed '*The Flower*' because I wanted to film the husband's visit, and his farewell.

THE GOODBYE LOOK

The steps taking him away from Leo ring out like bells tolling, heralding the death of their love.

Leaning against the corner of the landing, Leo/Marisa listens to the sound of Paco's footsteps and is paralysed. One by one, step by step Paco descends while the scene is played out in the real time it would take him to descend two whole floors of an old Madrid building, till he reaches the street. She endures the pain in an x-ray close-up.

It is a torrential, goodbye look.

I didn't want to take out a single image, a single step of the stairs, a single tear.

From that moment Leo and Paco walk in opposite directions. The same steps leading Paco to a new life push Leo towards death. Leo *has* to kill the love she feels for Paco, and the only way to do that is to kill herself – the physical form inseparable from that love.

When Leo goes to bed and closes her eyes to the world, after she's swallowed a lethal dose of Tranquimazin and her consciousness is clouding over, the telephone rings. It's her mother. She's had a row with Leo's sister (who lives on the city outskirts) and is ringing Leo to complain and to say goodbye. She wants to go back to her village, to escape from Madrid. 'I really wanted to say goodbye to you': the mother's voice, being recorded on the answering-machine, sounds depressed. Leo can hardly move, she opens her eyes. The telephone is in the lounge, and the lounge is far away, at the other end of the flat. An interminable passage separates it from the bedroom. Her mother's sad voice comes along the passage like a breath of air, reaches her bedroom door and shakes her daughter's weakened consciousness until it makes her react.

For years I've been tempted to make a film about my mother. The idea arose after a conversation with one of my sisters who remarked that Mum asked her to take her to a psychiatrist as she didn't want to go mad like her sister. I told my sister that Mum isn't mad, she just wants to talk. My sister pointed out, quite rightly, that she couldn't spend the whole day gossiping with her.

I'd never thought about it, but the conversation with my sister revealed to me the loneliness of my widowed mother and her roundabout search for an interlocutor. And I thought I could do something to help, and that it would be enough to sit opposite her and invite her to talk.

I've been discovering my mother quite by accident, listening to her while she talks to other people. For example, when I was preparing *Women* . . . I discovered that she'd dressed in black from the age of three to when she was past thirty.

We were in *El Corte Inglés*, looking for the dress she'd wear in *Women* . . . (she played a television announcer) when I heard her say to the shop assistant, who was serving us and insisting on dark colours, 'Give me something colourful, I don't want dark dresses, I've spent my life dressed in black. From the age of three, when my father died, until I was pregnant with this one – she pointed to

136

me – I tacked one period of mourning on to another.'

I said nothing, but the discovery shook me. I'd never imagined my mother had worn black while carrying me. I concluded I was the reaction against such an anti-natural tradition. Despite her black clothes, my mother was gestating her revenge on black within herself: yours truly, someone whose life would be shaped by colour, who would express itself through excess. When I heard her talking to the shop assistant, I understood my natural penchant for bright colours.

After talking to my sister I thought I should spend a few days with my mother and let her talk. I would listen. Summer was the ideal time because she spends it in our home village. I would go to the village and take a camera with me to record her words; I don't trust my memory.

But I never did it and I don't think I ever will. Something more complex than lethargy prevents me. The idea's still there. However, it comes and goes. Recently I've been reminded of it by two films: Erice's *The Quince Tree* and Kiarostami's *Through the Olive Trees*. Both films made me feel, once more, the need to meet up with my mother, listen to her, and construct a film from her words. I suppose it was the very moving, stark clarity of both films which reminded me of that need. If one day I were to take on the project about my mother, Erice and Kiarostami's films would be the natural, ideal stylistic reference points.

Instead of talking to her I became my own conversation partner and wrote (and filmed) *The Flower of My Secret*. I didn't go to my village in the summer, but made Leo accompany her mother to Almagro, a village thirty kilometres from mine which is a quintessential village on the plains of La Mancha. For their arrival I chose a street that recalls the street, as I remember it, where my mother lives, and for Chus Lampreave I wrote lines my own mother had spoken a thousand and one times.

I photographed the fields of infinite, red earth, stuck hard against the sky, the horizonless expanses of that La Mancha which marked my gaze as a child.

And women making lace in the patio, talking about the women who committed suicide by throwing themselves down wells; the final, black, crystalline mirror where suicidal Manchegans stare at themselves.

137

From the car I saw the ashen-coloured olive trees pass by, backstitching the infinite earth. As they get closer to Almagro, Chus recites 'My Village', a poem my mother used to recite (the last time she recited it was to the cameras of BBC2, in a documentary they made about me).

Leo recovers the will to live under the vine in the patio, whose roots, open to the wind, remind her where she comes from and of the first door she passed through on her way to the white street and its white blinding light.

LIKE A COW WITHOUT ITS BELL

ROOTS

Quite unconsciously, the initial 'husband's visit' became the pretext to make my most Manchegan film. The foresaken Leo's grief carried me back, without asking my permission, to my origins. And the effect was as unexpected as it was soothing. It's my hunch that the film about my mother's words is contained within *The Flower of My Secret*. I'm not referring to the drastic, gushing verbal diarrhoea of Chus Lampreave's character, but to something more essential and out of reach. An unconscious return to my roots. And the prime root is my mother.

I need to underline the fact that Almagro is the 'cradle of female needlework', the only place in La Mancha, which means 'the only place in the world', where women still sit out in the sun in order to make lace by hand. Sheets, curtains, table-cloths, handkerchiefs; they spend their whole lives doing this. There is one scene in particular which captures the film I didn't make about her: one as if through lace curtains: Jacinta, Leo's mother, walks over to the bed where her daughter is lying, pallid and lacking in appetite. The mother intuits Leo's drama, and laments: 'So sad, my love, so young yet already a cow without its bell!'

The comparison is not at all comic. Seeing Leo's shocked reaction, her mother explains: 'Lost, wandering, aimless, nobody keeping an eye on you . . . like me . . . I too am like a cow without its bell, but it's more normal at my age . . . That's why I want to live here, in the village. When a husband leaves his wife because he's died or gone off with another woman, it makes no odds . . . we must return to where we were born . . . Visit the local hermitage, chat on the doorstep with our neighbours, go to evening prayers with them, even though you're not a believer . . . because if not, we lose our way, like a cow without its bell . . .'

The cow-bell, like marriage, implies compromise, sometimes a heavy burden, but it also means, and that's what the mother is referring to, that you're not alone. A cow with a bell can't get lost, the farmhand will find it, guided by the ding-dong. The cow with a bell carries its own signal under its neck. After listening to her, Leo looks at her mother and sees herself reflected there. For different reasons, they are both alone. Without a cow-bell.

FEMALE SOLITUDE

I've finally reached the main theme of the film, of *The Flower of My Secret*, and also of the film that I would have created from my mother's words: solitude.

THE MAP

I was born in times that were bad for Spain, but very good for the cinema: the 1950s. I was very young when I first stepped into a village cinema. If my memory isn't playing tricks, it was like the one I recall in a sequence in *The Spirit of the Beehive*. Over time I've noticed how the memories I retain of films that have made an impact on me, don't usually match the original film, but are more about what they provoked in me when I saw them.

Apart from a chair, I also took to that village cinema a tin of charcoal to ward off the cold during the performance. Over the years, the heat from that improvised brazier has become the symbol of what the cinema meant for me in that period.

When I was eleven, in Extremadura, there was a cinema in the same street as the school where I was studying. At school, the priests were trying to deform my mind with their dogged religiosity. Unfortunately, a bit further up this street, transfixed in the cinema stalls, I found reconciliation with my world. A world of which I was sure I formed a part, dominated by perverse emotions. Very soon, at the age of eleven or twelve, I was forced to choose, and did so with the exuberance that accompanies inexperience. If I deserved to go to hell for seeing *Johnny Guitar*, *Picnic*, *Splendour in the Grass* or *Cat on a Hot Tin Roof*, I had no alternative but to accept such punishment. I didn't know what genes were but, undoubtedly, my genetic code was branded with fire as if I were a steer, branded with the stigma of the provincial film buff. I was much more sensitive to the voice of Tennessee Williams, springing from the lips of Liz Taylor, Paul Newman or Marlon Brando, than to the thick, slimy patter of my spiritual director. For my part, there wasn't a shadow of a doubt. The call of the light, projected into my eyes from the cinema screen, was much stronger than any other call.

What I didn't know was that decades later, some of these images projected on the screens of my childhood, would bear my signature and would be marked by those first films in which my real spiritual director was Tennessee Williams.

AROUND AND ABOUT THE BED

In a love story the bed is very important, though relative, as lovers need only their bodies to express themselves as such, but in a story of love going cold the bed is essential. Infrequent use is eloquent testimony and the best thermometer to measure the temperature of relationships.

In *The Flower of My Secret* there's only one Big Bed Scene between Leo and her husband, during which they never lie down and the Bed stands only as witness.

Paco has just returned from a trip abroad, Leo leads him into the bedroom, not letting him talk, devouring him with her fingers, but he really wants to shower, and uses the sweat from the journey as a pretext – Leo and her husband circle around the bed, as she undoes his shirt one button at a time, to an incantation of her immediate desires, to the rhythm of the undone buttons: 'First have a shower, as that appeals so, (*first button done*) . . . then we'll fuck (*second button*) . . . a short rest (*button*) . . . then we'll fuck again (*button*) and then, God knows! (*fifth button and off with his shirt*)' Everything on the edge of the bed, as if they were on the edge of an altar. An altar to be transformed into an abyss as deep as the Grand Canyon, and equally dangerous if one falls into the void.

After his shower (during which Leo waits towel in hand, eyeing him hungrily), a vicious argument breaks out, suddenly, like a tropical storm. Paco explains he doesn't have a day's leave, as he promised her, but only two hours, after which he must return to the airport. Leo bellows her frustration. But Paco is a soldier, and tells her: 'I don't have to explain to you what my duty is.' 'You're my husband,' Leo points out, 'do I have to explain what your duty is to me?'

The argument flares up in the bedroom, while Paco's putting on clean pants and a vest. The Bed is witness to the huge abyss opening up between the couple. Silent, intact, enormous, the Bed only welcomes Leo's buttocks when she sits with her back to Paco. Driven by the monotony of pain harboured over months, Leo reveals her own opinion on the Peace Mission that is separating them: 'You went off to sort out a war, fleeing from the one you had here, in your own home, and in that war I'm the only victim.' Leo stays seated, her back to him, unable to see Paco leaving the bedroom, creeping into the bathroom. She doesn't realize he's not even listening to her. Leo goes from being a Tennessee Williams character, one of those strong women with right on their side even when they get it hopelessly wrong, to a character from Cocteau: a woman abandoned, even when she has the object of desire in front of her, because the object in question has gone to sleep (the indifference of Beauty) or isn't there.

I rehearsed the scene with the actors to the point of torture. After this process my only problem was *what* to put over the bed. This will sound absurd, but it wasn't purely an aesthetic problem. The image placed above the bedhead dominates our bedroom, watches over our sleep, stands guard by the entrance to our intimacy, symbolizes something one believes in, something inspiring respect, it shelters and protects us, it is a sacred space. As my characters are not fervent believers, it was a delicate matter deciding on the image to place above their bedhead. I finally decided to hang a large map of Spain there, in a handsome gilt frame. One of those maps, with sky-blue seas, in front of which we would be stood to have our school photo taken.

I never had the opportunity to have that photo taken. I feel as if it was snatched from me; a real treat which every child had a right to. I think the day it was my turn I couldn't go to school because I was moving with my family to Extremadura, in search of prosperity.

A priest-run school, a bad religious education, geography and cinema, all thrown together in my life like chick-peas, bacon and potatoes in a Madrid stew.

My troubled relationship with geography continued in the school in Extramadura. All the Salesians Fathers ever taught me was fear and how to sing exquisite Masses in Latin. I was the soloist in a well-known children's choir. To enable me to rehearse, the priests excused me from geography lessons and at the end of the year they passed me on the nod. I grew up convinced the universe was a fantasy and so when, fifteen years later, I started frantically travelling, I went blindly, never knowing how far it was to the places I was visiting. I often wondered if they existed, was always surprised when they did.

I mention all this to explain to what extent geography and maps have always meant something wondrous, mysterious and abstract in my eyes. That's why I put a map over Leo and Paco's bed.

One only feels protected by what one doesn't know and perhaps that's the real point of religion, a fascination for the unknown. Something we lack or didn't get at the right time. I've deprived God and his saints of their rightful place, and put in their stead a political map of Spain. That map (and that knowledge), which I never had access to as a child, was summoned up to preside over the scene that gave birth to *The Flower of My Secret*.

THE ROSE-TINTED AND THE BLACK

The colour of literary genres isn't just a label that pigeon-holes and simplifies them. The colour of literature is as important and as informative as the colour of a woman's hair; even if it's dyed. A woman becomes more authentic the closer she resembles the woman of her dreams.

There are blondes, brunettes and redheads. They are distinguished not only by the colour of their hair, but by behaviour, sensibility and style. If a blonde doesn't behave the way blondes should, she's condemned to failure and disaffection. She can only create confusion inside and outside of herself.

If a writer of a *série rose* novel, who's lost her way or is grief-stricken, contemplates herself in the black mirror of reality, she is looking the wrong way (a writer's vision is of the essence) and has crossed the frontier dividing two genres which are such opposites and near neighbours, the *rose* and the *noir*.

Séries noires detectives and *séries roses* heroines are characters with more affinities than differences. Philip Marlowe and Sam Spade are two hopelessly sentimental guys. They are saved from sentimentality by an alcoholic cynicism which is justified by the disappointments they've suffered. Cynicism becomes another cloak beneath which they hide their bleeding hearts of gold. Their disappointments have more to do with melodrama than with crime fiction. They also have different critical attitudes towards the society in which they're destined to live. Social conscience is absent, if not banned, from the rose-tinted universe. But not from melodrama. In fact, melodrama with a social conscience goes by the name of neo-realism.

Although related, the *série rose* must not be confused with melodrama. All rose-tinted novels are melodramatic, but not all melodramas are rose-tinted.

It is also true that all genres, in literature and film, cross into each other. More and more they influence each other, divide and sub-divide, mix. This general, generous promiscuity of the genres (eclecticism, mestizo hybridity) is characteristic of a lazy century drawing up its balance sheet before it passes into history.

Let's return to our protagonist. The change that takes place in Leo's life is about a change of colour, and also about the colours of life and writing running together. At the beginning she's writing rose-tinted novels although her life is very sombre. At the end it's just the opposite, her perspectives on life are much warmer, not exactly rose-tinted (that would be unreal), but certainly orange-hued, like the sky at twilight or the fire in an open fireplace. As for her writing, although this isn't made clear in the film, I can reveal it's probably black and zany, inspired by the reality that fills the pages of the daily papers. Leo has several folders full of newspaper cuttings of extraordinary real-life stories. In *The Flower* . . . they're almost invisible, but they are on the top of her desk. I put them there on purpose.

The heroine of the *série rose* and the anti-hero of the *série noire* are similar in that they are by themselves at the start, but they finish up quite differently. At the end, the anti-hero remains sad and lonely. (Basically I think anti-heroes enjoy chaos and solitude, and a woman would end up organizing their lives and homes. That's precisely the difference between an anti-hero and an everyday guy.)

The rose-tinted heroine, on the other hand, by the end of the novel has always got a partner, sometimes an unsatisfactory one, but that doesn't matter. In the *série rose* loneliness is fine to begin with, but outlawed at the end.

THE GREY AND THE BLUE

There are films we have heard so much about, that turn up so often in newspapers and on television channels, you feel you've see them lots of times. In reality you've never seen them, or perhaps just once, and that was so long ago you might as well not have seen them.

That happened to me with *Casablanca*. I'd seen it twenty years ago, but was tired of hearing about it and couldn't be bothered to go and see it again. However, by chance, I did see it again two years ago, and it was a real eye-opener.

I noted down odd sentences, I usually do if I'm at home. I'm a disaster as a film buff, I never remember sentences which strike me and which I could use to effect on everybody else. My notes aren't very helpful because I lose them within days. That wasn't the case with the notes I took on *Casablanca*. The following day I got a phone call from *El Mundo* asking me to write something on the cinema; they were celebrating the birthday of their film section, Cinelandia. I decided to talk about the importance of clothes in films, and had recourse to a Bogart dialogue in *Casablanca* that I'd noted down on a yellow Post-it. On their first reunion, Ingrid Bergman asks Bogart if he remembers the last time they met, in Paris. Bogart looks at her woodenly and replies: 'I remember every detail. (It was the day the Germans occupied Paris.) The Germans wore grey, you wore blue.'

Impossible to be more emotional, yet Bogart was simply commenting on the colour of the clothing. Apart from carrying bodies, clothes carry emotions. Carry and communicate.

Months later *Kika* was premièred in London. The party for the *première* was turned into a pretext for raising money for a foundation that helped Aids sufferers. An auction of clothes from modern designers (Gaultier, Mugler, V. Westwood, etc) and a number of presents from famous people was organized. It was the usual well-meaning but God-awful party; all the trendies in town turned up. The only serious character was the fellow presiding over the auction, a real auctioneer from Sotheby's. I had donated one of the marvellous credits which Juan Gatti made for *Women*

. . . In fact it was my credit, as screenplay writer and director. I supposedly donated the original, but I have to say it was only a copy. Under glass you couldn't tell. I gave it a huge, hand-made gilt frame that cost me a hundred thousand pesetas. What was really valuable (apart from my gesture) was the frame, but obviously I didn't mention that.

After giving thirty or so interviews in English at the top of my voice, and amid the sweat and the furore, an incisive, no-bullshit journalist asked whether fashion was really any more than a game to allow whores and queers to feel 'divine'. Before I replied I looked him straight in the eye, dead calm, knowing I was right and knew how to communicate it. Once again I had recourse to Bogart and his opportune comment on German grey and Ingrid Bergman blue. I told him that in films clothes aren't just there to make girls look pretty, but define the period when the action takes place, establish the genre and the social class of the characters. And if that weren't enough, as I demonstrated with Bogart's phrase, clothes can carry deep emotional symbolism.

Months later, into the third or fourth version of *The Flower* . . ., it struck me that, under the influence of alcohol, Angel would throw discretion to the wind and have recourse to Bogart's words to express the emotion he was holding back: '. . . the Germans wore grey and you wore blue' he finally says to Leo, after asking her whether she remembered *Casablanca*, etc.

Leo looks at him startled. They're alone in the huge Plaza Mayor. A solitude that seems more theatrical than real. Leo wonders what her friend means by those words.

'You wore blue the day you were running from your life and collided with mine', Angel replies, his voice choked with tears. Leo moves away from him, with a feeling of distaste. She's been trying to forget that moment for months (it was the day her husband left her for ever, she hadn't thought about it but it was true she was wearing blue jeans and a blue coat) Angel, however, can never forget that. It is one of my favourite scenes. And I owe it mainly to Bogart's words.

It was a lucky break deciding to see *Casablanca* again. Sometimes making a simple note on a yellow Post-it implies an investment as extraordinary as it is unpredictable. I had never turned a simple note to so much advantage.

150

CREDITS

CAST

LEO	Marisa Paredes
ANGEL	Juan Echanove
PACO	Imanol Arias
ROSA	Rossy de Palma
JACINTA	Chus Lampreave
BETTY	Carmen Elias
ANTONIO	Joaquín Cortes
BLANCA	Manuela Vargas

CREW

Written and directed by	Pedro Almodóvar
Executive producer	Agustín Almodóvar
Director of production	Esther García
Director of photography	Alfonso Beato
Editor	José Salcedo
Sound	Bernardo Menz
Design	Wolfgang Burmann
Costume	Hugo Mezcua
Make-up	Miguel López Pelegrín
Hair	Antonio Panizza
Original score	Alberto Iglesias

SONGS

'Tonada de luna llena'
Performed by Caetano Veloso

'En el último trago'
Performed by Chavela Vargas

'Ay amor'
Performed by Bola de Nieve

'Soleá'
Performed by Miles Davis

NOTE ON THE TRANSLATOR

Peter Bush is Reader in Literary Translation at Middlesex University. He has translated the work of Juan Goytisolo, Juan Carlos Onetti, Senel Paz and Luis Sepúlveda. He won an Outstanding Translation for 1994 Award from the American Literary Translators Association.